THE POOR MAN'S GUIDE TO TRIVIA COLLECTING

By John Mebane

Books Relating to the Civil War: A Priced Check-List
Treasure at Home
New Horizons in Collecting
The Coming Collecting Boom
What's New That's Old
The Poor Man's Guide to Antique Collecting
The Complete Book of Collecting Art Nouveau
Collecting Nostalgia
Best Sellers in Antiques
The Poor Man's Guide to Trivia Collecting

THE
POOR MAN'S

GUIDE TO
TRIVIA
COLLECTING

By John Mebane

Doubleday & Company, Inc.
Garden City, New York
1975

Library of Congress Cataloging in Publication Data

Mebane, John, 1901–
    The poor man's guide to trivia collecting.

    Bibliography: p. 182.
    Includes index.
    1. Art industries and trade—Collectors and collecting.   I. Title.
NK1125.M3595   700'.75
ISBN 0-385-01947-5
Library of Congress Catalog Card Number 73–22805

ACKNOWLEDGMENTS

MANY PEOPLE helped with the preparation of this book, and the author is grateful to them all, and particularly to the Freeman family of Smyrna, Georgia. Bill Freeman took all of the photographs in this book that are not credited to other photographers or collections, and his wife, Jan, spent a good many hours in correlating and arranging the illustrative material.

Sincere thanks are due also to numerous antiques dealers and astute collectors for their advice on what to include herein and for their help with values. The author would also like to express his appreciation to the following, who provided advice, photographs, or other assistance:

The Antiques Journal and the Babka Publishing Company, Dubuque, Iowa; Rita Brand, Forest Hills, New York; Mr. and Mrs. L. D. Brodsky, Farmington, Missouri; Bert Curbo, Westwego, Louisiana; Herman C. Carter, Tulsa, Oklahoma; Mrs. Robert E. Carter, III, Charlottesville, Virginia; Ed L. Chandler, Doraville, Georgia; *Collector's World*, Conroe, Texas; Sam A. Cousley and The Cousley Collections, Englewood, New Jersey; Delta Air Lines, Inc., Atlanta, Georgia; Detroit Historical Museum, Detroit, Michigan; Samuel T. Freeman & Company, Philadelphia; Shelly Goldstein, Woodland Hills, California; Stan Gores, Fond du Lac, Wisconsin; Historical Society of Buster Brown Comics and Marketing and Miss Frances L. Charman, Curator, New York City; Gladys Hollander, Long Beach, California; Mrs. Harold H. Howe, Sanford, Florida; Graham Hunter, West Orange, New Jersey; Grace Kendrick, Fallon, Nevada; C. R. Maize, Somerset, Pennsylvania.

Also, P. M. McClintock, Franklin, Pennsylvania; Mrs. Wanda McPeters, Hobbs, New Mexico; Richard O. Miller, Hodson, Massachusetts; North American Rockwell, El Segundo, California; Bill Poese, Jefferson, Ohio; Kenneth W. Rendell, Autographs, Somerville, Massachusetts; Paul C. Richards, Autographs, Bridgewater, Massachusetts; Jerry Rillahan, Worland, Wyoming; Floyd and Marion Rinhart, Melbourne Beach, Florida; Frank Rochat, Carlstadt, New

Jersey; *Spinning Wheel*, Hanover, Pennsylvania; Steinfeld Antiques, Westfield, Connecticut; Francis R. Teeple, Greene, Iowa; George Theofiles (Miscellaneous Man), Baltimore; Charles (Chuck) Wooley, Peoria, Illinois; and Pete Zarilla, New York City.

Some of the illustrations in this book came from early trade catalogues, some issued by firms that are no longer in business, but among those that are and who graciously gave permission to use their illustrations are Americana Interstate Corporation, Mundelein, Illinois; Belknap Hardware and Manufacturing Company, Louisville, Kentucky; Bennett Brothers, Inc., Chicago; and Harry Greenwold, Wallenstein-Mayer Company, Cincinnati.

CONTENTS

THE POOR MAN'S GUIDE TO TRIVIA COLLECTING

WHATEVER HAPPENED TO BERNARD PALISSY?

YOU REMEMBER HIM, of course—the first of the great naturalists. Palissy is the fellow who created those fantastic pieces of pottery adorned with snakes, lizards, fish, shells, and plant life after forming molds with living specimens. Stylistic ornament was not for him; you can look at a Palissy plate and see that a snail is a snail is a snail and not a snapping turtle in disguise.

Palissy had his problems. He gave up surveying to try his hand at glassmaking, but, being virtually penniless—or, as they said in his native France, without a sou to his name—he used his furniture and the flooring of his house for fuel, thereby losing what little credit he had since many folks thought him a bit touched. But he was a persistent fellow and turned from glass to pottery, finally perfecting some remarkable glazes and a type of relief pottery with naturalistic ornaments known to connoisseurs as *rustiques figulines*. He managed to attain considerable prestige and turn out some masterpieces in a workshop erected for him in the gardens of the Tuileries before being tossed into the bastille at Bucy, where he died near the tail end of the sixteenth century.

Some millionaires were able to acquire some Palissy pieces last century—although it is reported that a few of them were stuck with imitations made in Portugal or by the Parisian M. Barbizet—but even millionaires would be hard-pressed to purchase them today.

But of course much the same thing has happened to period Chippendale bookcases, choice signed pieces from the reigns of Louis XIV or his two Louis successors (although a Louis XV mahogany and kingwood marquetry table signed by Jean-François Oeben, et al., brought only $410,000 at a Parke-Bernet sale in late 1971), Tiffany "Apple Blossom" lamps, and many other antiques that one could have picked up a scant quarter of a century ago for a sum equivalent to a handsome year's salary.

The trouble is that not too many people are making antiques any longer, while the number of people wanting to collect them for either love or money has increased enormously. Now, it is obvious that not very many of these novice collectors can afford any prime antiques dating back to the eighteenth century or earlier, at least not without giving up some other pleasures such as drinking or smoking or chasing women (or men). But if there is anything more difficult than paying this year's taxes on last year's salary, it is turning off a person who has been turned on to collecting.

For generations the Establishment has resented the intrusion of the hoi polloi into the circle of antique collectors, and those who could afford it have devoted considerable energy to running prices to such a point as to discourage the peasantry. In this—alas!—they have succeeded remarkably well. But although the intimidating combination of scarcity and high price has cut the props from under many an aspiring but impecunious collector of antiques, it has by no means discouraged collecting per se.

What is happening right now is that new types of collectible objects are emerging, and they will continue to emerge in the years ahead. Scores of objects made in the long Victorian period attained this category some years ago, and quite a number of these objects are now legitimate antiques, at least from the standpoint of age. But hundreds of more recent articles are now moving into this circle, and their values are climbing rapidly. Certain of these have been "discovered" by astute explorers of city dumps and charity bazaars, others by those intrepid adventurers who search the bins and miscellaneous receptacles of second-hand stores or whose fingers have walked the pages of merchandise catalogues now mustering with age.

Since about 1960 a number of new categories of collectibles that have by no means reached the status of antiquity have been popularized in the pages of various collector periodicals, excluding the most elite. Readers will recognize some of them since they range from Depression glass to Zanesville pottery and from late nineteenth- or early twentieth-century nonmechanical banks to the sinuous creations of Art Nouveau.

But there are literally dozens of other categories that are just now coming to the notice of enterprising collectors because they are nostalgic reminders of an era that remains entrapped in the secret crevices of memory, and at the moment, at least, nostalgia is the name of the game. We are engulfed by a wave of homesickness for the past—a longing to reach back and touch the sweet moments of our younger days, to conjure up somehow the baubles that once enchanted us, the catchpenny gift that once was treasured beyond the reach of gold, a twinkling vision caught in the corner of an eye along some alleyway at dusk. And it is for this very reason (together with the general inaccessibility of rare antiques) that many of these things, no matter how trivial we may consider them, constitute excellent potentials for investment. Many of those that we will consider in this book have not yet come into demand so that there is no wild scrambling for them and thus no spiraling of prices in general, though both are likely to come.

It is upon these relatively trivial yet potentially profitable objects, nearly all of them products of the machine age, that this book focuses. Some of them are destined to become the antiques of the future so that the intrepid collector who purchases them at current low prices may profit, though of course not so handsomely as those who inherit Hepplewhite desks or steal Hitchcock fancy chairs by cozening needy but unwitting widows who would not know a zooid from a zoetrope.

There is a boom in trivia in the making, and those who first encounter collectible trivia in this volume may get in on the ground floor of a motley but exciting market destined to rise. Of course, there is junk, and junk will always be with us; but what was junk to our parents may not necessarily be junk to our children. Nor will what is junk to the connoisseur necessarily be junk to the adventurous collector who knows that a host of objects fashioned or used by his grandparents may be as remote and therefore as fascinating for his children as are the artifacts of Herculaneum to him. It is a phenomenon of our times that the johnny come-latelies to the fold of collectibles sometimes ascend in value as rapidly—and in some cases more rapidly—than traditional antiques despite a world of difference in basic and intrinsic values.

There is no guarantee that all of the objects about which tips are presented here will rise swiftly in value; but, in the judgment of both dealers and collectors seasoned in what we call the "new antiques," most of them are likely to. Certainly, for those of unabashed spirit, they will be fun to ferret out and either to retain as the basis of a permanent collection or to hold for a spell with a view toward profit.

Take, for example, the case of Art Nouveau. Furniture, glass, ceramics, and examples of the graphic arts produced in this once audacious style, which flourished in the 1890s and lingered until the days of World War I, were consigned in the postwar period to junkyards and attics—only to be rediscovered by collectors a few years ago. Not only did the unsalable sell, but prices took wing.

And so it is now happening with Art Deco, that brash intruder of the twenties and thirties, which was forgotten by the forties, and vaguely remembered only as "Art Moderne." Now it is being disinterred and groomed for its Second Coming. Thus far it has been chiefly the loftier examples of Art Deco that have been making a splash—but there is more to come.

Values assigned to the objects here are based on (1) prices at which some are now being traded and (2) the collective experience, coupled with guesswork, of both individuals and dealers who are seeking something new under the sun to collect. But because they are new to the collecting field, their prices will fluctuate, sometimes quite widely, from one area and one dealer to another until they are traded in sufficient volume to enable more realistic guidelines to be established. Certainly many current values should be well under the market a few years hence.

In some cases it has not been possible to list a group of prices because there has been thus far insufficient commerce in these categories. A reasonable price range has been suggested instead. And in other cases in which there has been an extremely wide variation in prices for the same or similar objects, prices have been averaged to arrive at the figures listed.

Although the prices that are cited have been culled from scores of sources and every effort has been made to arrive at fair figures, there is no guarantee that these will be the prices at which everyone can sell or buy, the major reason being a rapid change in many of them, almost invariably upward.

I welcome suggestions from readers but regret that I cannot engage in correspondence relating to values.

ADVERTISING MEMENTOS

THAT IRRESISTIBLE GIMMICK—something free for nothing—may not have lured the gullible from time immemorial, but it comes close. The advertising profession has utilized the giveaway (free, or almost) for decades on behalf of its clients, and the practice is continuing unabated into the waning years of the twentieth century. Those who have not at some time been the recipient of advertising giveaways have obviously lived hermitlike.

The men who sat in ivory towers and dreamed up these slight but tolerable windfalls to shower upon the populace could not have visualized the day that these trifles would be fervently sought in the marketplace. But that day has arrived, and advertising giveaways now constitute a choice collectible category of their own.

Some, such as beverage serving trays and mirrors, have so caught the public fancy that many of their prices do not constitute bargains, and we will not deal with those here except to mention in passing that they are sought and to cite a few values.

Actually, collectible objects associated with efforts to sell goods and services range from alphabet plates to zircons, and today's collector is best advised to pick a specific category and stick with it.

Certain areas that have become crowded include promotional objects associated with that soft drink that made the phrase "the pause that refreshes" famous. An 1899 tray a scant 9½ inches in diameter and bearing a likeness of Hilda Clark will set you back—if it's in pristine condition—about $1,000, and even one issued in 1920 portraying a demure lass in a garden will fetch over a hundred. Shelly Goldstein of Woodland Hills, California, collected so many objects associated with the promotion of Coca-Cola that he wrote a book about them (*Coca-Cola Collectibles,* 1971) in which he assigns to a 1904 bookmark lettered "Coca-Cola" and adorned with a full-length depiction of Lillian Russell a value of $50, and to a 3-foot-high 1923 tin sign in the shape of a bottle a value of $75. The collector of Coca-Cola items may also find of interest a chapter devoted to them in my book *Collecting Nostalgia* (Arlington House, 1972).

But except for some special cases, the field of advertising mementos, particularly the giveaways, is wide open, with astute dealers and collectors alike agreeing that prices are likely to rise for some years to come.

We will limit the discussion in this chapter to a few categories that have not yet been belabored and that appear to offer a good potential.

Lettered or pictorial match safes and cigar clippers with an advertising message are close kin, and they constitute an intriguing field for the collector. Both were issued as promotional gimmicks by scores of firms. Match safes of sterling and of nickel silver have been turned out since the latter part of the nineteenth century by the carload. Virtually all are collectible, but those lettered with the name of a company and given away to win customers will interest the collector of advertising memorabilia. Silver and silver-plate manufacturers turned out "stock" designs on which any advertiser could have his name engraved or stamped. The same held true for pocket cigar cutters; but in addition to these, the counter cigar cutters, sometimes combined with lighting devices and lettered with the name of a business firm—usually a tobacco processor—are also collectible.

It must be borne in mind that the price of silver in the early years of this century had not attained today's level and even sterling-silver match safes were available at wholesale prices of $2.00 to $2.25 and sterling cigar cutters were being offered at about a dollar. Quantity purchases brought these figures down considerably.

The match safes were crafted in a great many designs, which adds to the challenge of collecting them. Many boasted floral motifs, and these were stylized during the years of commercial Art Nouveau so that their stems flowed sinuously around the edges of the case. Some of the Art Nouveau era safes were embossed with heads of ladies with flowing hair—a favorite motif of designers of the period. Others bore on the face of their cases likenesses of grim Indians, friendly canines, timorous maidens, and—for the sport—ladies clad in nothing more than a smile. In a category close kin to the advertising match safes were those made for fraternal organizations ranging from Masons to the Benevolent and Protective Order of Elks and decorated with their insignia.

Silver-plated cases with enameled decoration instead of embossing were wholesaling early in this century at under half a dollar each, and the majority of the promotional safes are plated rather than sterling. During World War I, with patriotism at fever pitch, many match safes with an enameled representation of the United States flag were made, and a substantial number were bought by commercial establishments that added their names to the cases.

Counter-type cigar cutters were found in all tobacco and many general stores last century and early in the present one. These were used, of course, as were the

Early twentieth-century match safes. First two on top row are gold-filled; one at right in center has an enameled flag, and the others are sterling silver or plated silver. B.P.O. Elks safe shown at bottom right.

7

pocket sizes, to clip the sealed ends from cigars before the latter acquired a hole in their heads. These now are scarce and relatively high priced (they were banned in some localities years ago as being unsanitary). Major producers were the Brunhoff Manufacturing Company, Cincinnati, and the Erie Specialty Company, Erie, Pennsylvania, and they were lettered with the names of cigar and general tobacco manufacturers, many of which are no longer in business.

Far more abundant for collectors are the pocket cutters, and these are cropping up now at many flea markets, interesting if not important reminders of a fairly recent past. Occasionally, too, one will encounter at antique shops small flat cutters intended for use atop desks.

The small desk cutters are particularly interesting because of the shapes in which they were made, including owls, crying babies, animals, cannon, and other objects. Most pocket cutters are quite small. A typical type consists of a metal case with a hole on one side into which the cigar tip was inserted. A blade behind the hole was activated to clip the cigar tip. Another type resembled a miniature pair of scissors riveted together at one end and with a cutting blade that was operated by closing together two finger inserts in much the same way one uses scissors for cutting.

Sterling-silver cigar cutters from the turn of the century. One in center on top row is decorated with a small diamond.

Sterling-silver pocket cutters sold from $1.50 to $5.00 half a century ago. Some also were made of gold, and costly ones were set with precious, including diamonds, or semiprecious stones. Some fine and costly ones were offered by exclusive jewelry establishments. Also available were boxed sets that contained a pocket knife and a cigar cutter and sometimes a match safe too. Albert Brothers, wholesale jewelers of Cincinnati, offered a choice three-piece set in its 1914 catalogue for $50, which in those days was no meager sum. Tobacco merchants purchased the less expensive pocket cutters in bulk, had their names engraved or imprinted on them, and offered them to customers.

One of the advantages of collecting match safes and pocket cigar cutters is their size, small enough to enable one to assemble a large variety that can be displayed in a relatively small area.

Advertising paperweights were once made in great profusion. These, too, will interest collectors of advertising giveaways and even the less fastidious collectors of paperweights in general. Most of the early handmade glass weights produced by such famous factories as those of Baccarat, St. Louis, Clichy, France, and a number of English and American glasshouses, have long since reached price levels that place them beyond the pale of the indigent. In addition, there are scores of types of nonadvertising novelty paperweights that afford a rich field for the average collector.

A large percentage of the commercial giveaways were illustrations or merely the name and address of a mercantile establishment or a service agency imbedded in a heavy, flat, oblong piece of glass. Some of the illustrations used were photographs of store exteriors or urban or rural scenes, many of which are now of historic importance and merit preservation. Other giveaways were of metal in various shapes, some embossed with a scene, others merely lettered. Later ones were fashioned of clear plastic in which some type of advertising message was inserted.

Novelty paperweights abounded, early in this century, and some are truly fascinating. Among these are gold-plated weights in the shape of such animals as alligators and turtles and usually measuring about three to five inches in length. These were available at the turn of this century for less than a dollar. They're now valued a good bit higher though they are still by no means expensive. In the 1890s, Bloomingdale Brothers of New York City offered a small silver-plated winged cupid figure as a paperweight for a mere $.18 cents to which mail order customers added $.12 cents for postage. Small gold-plated horses, lions, and greyhounds were offered as either paperweights or "cabinet ornaments" in the 1902 catalogue of Oskamp, Nolting & Company of Cincinnati at prices of a dollar each.

Intriguing novelty and advertising paperweights continued to be turned out for some years thereafter, sold inexpensively, but their values will be up today. One example is a rather late globe weight with a figure of Santa Claus inside. When the weight was lifted and shaken, "snow" drifted down on Santa, and presumably these were popular as Christmas gifts. They originally wholesaled for half a dollar or less, but some have recently been tendered on the "antiques" market at $15.

Advertising thermometers have been around for a long time and those in figural shapes may take off on a price spiral any time now. They have been used through the years to promote soft drinks, beer, cigarettes, and other treats for the thirsty or jaded. These are usually found in the shapes of bottles or cigarette packages, lettered with the name of the product being promoted and containing

Novelty paperweights. From left, top row: gold-plated lizard, 1900; gold-leafed fish globe, 1940; silver-plated cupid, 1892. Second row: gold-plated turtle, 1900; bronzed metal pyramidal weight, late nineteenth century. Bottom: silver-plated steer on base by M. S. Benedict Manufacturing Company, ca. 1904; nickel-plated revolver, 1934.

a simple and inexpensive thermometer tube attached to the tin figural shape. Larger ones, some measuring more than two feet high, were made for manufacturers or processors and presented to establishments handling their products, to be attached to a wall inside or outside the building. The smaller ones—about a foot or less to as much as 18 inches high—were made for giveaways to retail customers.

Thousands of these are still around somewhere and can undoubtedly be picked up for a dollar or so, but a few astute dealers already are on the lookout for them and are offering them at $5.00 to $25.

Like the paperweights, many fascinating novelty thermometers were manufactured for sale and these also are collectible. Prices will certainly start to climb as collectors of relatively trivial objects discover them. Most of these were thermometers mounted on fancy and figural stands of brass or other metals or glass. One brass stand featured a cupid beneath a parasol. Another was made with a case in the shape of a stirrup mounted on an oval metal base. Others featured cast-metal figural adjuncts, animals and humans among them, usually mounted on the base, making them kissing kin of the figural napkin rings that are now the delight of so many collectors. Many stands combined a figural base with a figural finial, the latter including miniature replicas of such figures as Shakespeare, Napoleon, and Prince Albert. The figural thermometers are much more difficult to find than the advertising variety, and their prices will be considerably higher.

Before leaving this subject, I should mention that clinical thermometers in decorated cases remain sleepers right now. Cases may be sterling silver with engine-turned silver chains, gold-filled or mother-of-pearl, and many were lavishly decorated by chasing or embossing.

One interesting figural thermometer I acquired is in the shape of a small wooden bear with an oval thermometer imbedded in its side. It probably retailed originally for about a dollar, but currently should be worth about five times that.

Advertising thermometers in the collection of Francis R. Teeple, Greene, Iowa.

Unless the tubes have been broken and the mercury has leaked out, a surprisingly large number of the old thermometers remain fairly reliable today. They can be displayed by hanging them along a wall or placing them on a shelf in the den or playroom.

Those interested in earlier types of thermometers and in barometers will find some discussion of them in my *The Coming Collecting Boom,* published in 1968 (A. S. Barnes and Company).

At a time when interest in the graphic arts generally seems to be at a peak, a number of collectors are turning their attention to reproductions of paintings and to other prints, particularly those in color, that were used by certain businesses to engender good will.

Breweries liked to present prints of undraped ladies, to be hung behind the bar. Some of the early ones fetch truly handsome prices today. In fact, reproductions of "art" in the form of nudes or semi-nudes will bring higher prices today than any other type of advertising art, and the purchasers seem to be universally male. Particularly high prices have been paid for these nudes in large and ornate frames, and even some of today's taverns for male customers are acquiring them for use in their establishments.

But advertising and promotional pictorials were by no means limited to depictions of unclad maidens. Famous paintings of the past were reproduced in quantity by manufacturers or processors and presented to their retail customers for display. Others were acquired by retail businesses and such firms as insurance companies for presentation to their customers. These included reproductions of Currier & Ives prints; many amateur collectors purchased reproductions in the belief that they were originals. Sometimes it is easy to distinguish the originals from the later reproductions by their size. But then you can't carry around either in your head or a memorandum tablet the specific sizes in which all the original Currier & Ives were printed. However, those interested will find of much help an article, "Currier & Ives—and How to Identify Originals," by John and Barbara Rudisill in the November 1972 issue of *The Antiques Journal.*

Most of these promotional prints are trifles, but indications are that prices will soon start upward.

As was pointed out earlier, other objects associated with advertising are collectible, including serving and change trays, small mirrors, hanging signs of all types, counter-top placards, oversized replicas of display bottles and other containers and products. (Very early signs have been collected by dedicated individuals and museums for years and are scarce and costly; more available are pictorial metal signs from the late years of the nineteenth and early years of the twentieth centuries. An embossed tin sign in the shape of a Negro boy holding an advertisement for a clothing firm and public bath between his hands and measuring 40×48 inches in size was offered recently at the rather astonishing price of $1,250!)

Optician's sign of 1905 with carved eye pupils standing out in relief. Sign measures 3 feet long and was gilded.

Current prices of some of the objects discussed in this chapter follow, and, although I have not discussed them in detail here, I am also listing prices for advertising mirrors, trays, placards, posters, signs, and some display items, since there are already many collectors of these.

Typical current values of some of the objects discussed in this chapter follow:

CIGAR CLIPPERS AND MATCH SAFES

Cigar cutter, counter-top, gold-lettered red glass reading "Chamber of Commerce Quality Cigars," 8×6 inches $49.00

Cigar cutter, counter-top, small, iron, advertising Declarencia Havana Cigars $35.00

Cigar cutter, counter-top, picture of Indian behind cellophane $25.00

Cigar cutter, counter-top, iron donkey, plunger type; tail lifts cigars $150.00

Cigar cutter, counter-top, small, key-wound, glass, marked "Y & B" $50.00

Cigar cutter, pocket, metal in shape of shoe $9.50

Cigar cutter, pocket, metal, advertising Havana cigars $10.50

Cigar cutter, pocket, metal with match holder, raised deer decor $9.50

Cigar cutter, pocket, ivory with silver end, advertising beer $13.00

Cigar cutter, pocket, brass clipper and knife, advertising Blogett & Orswell Co. $15.00

Match safe, advertising Moxie, tin $38.00

Match safe, advertising Schlitz Beer, with cigar cutter $15.00

Match safe, advertising Pan-American Exposition, nickel-plated brass $12.50

Match safe, advertising men's wear and dated 1904, with cigar cutter $13.95

Match safe, advertising Michigan Stove Company, frog finial, iron $18.00

Match safe, advertising Old Connecticut fire insurance, hinged turtle, iron $17.00

Match safe, advertising Diamond Matches, striker bottom, brass $12.50

Match safe, patriotic, with U.S. flag, nickel-plated brass $8.50

Brass, flat, advertising Chalmers Motor Car Company $10.00

Brass, in shape of shoe, advertising shoes, 3 inches high $12.50

Brass, in shape of 5-inch-long spike, advertising dredging and dock corporation $6.00

Brass, advertising door locks, lettering on one side, illustration on reverse $7.50

Cast iron, 3 inches long, advertising cable company $12.50

Cast iron, 2½ inches long, painted silver, advertising Hoosier Owl $10.00

Cast iron, 2½ inches long, hand-engraved on one side, advertising cutters' tools $8.00

Cast iron, in shape of fire helmet, advertising insurance $18.00

Composition, 4½ inches long, advertising cement $10.00

Composition, in shape of bag, advertising concrete mixes $2.50

Glass, oval, 4⅜ inches long, advertising stoves and lamps $4.95

Glass, rectangular, mirror back, 4¼×2¾ inches, advertising The Marble Palace, Newport, R.I. $4.95

Glass, lettered "Coke is Coca-Cola" in blue $65.00

Glass, 3¼×2½ inches, lettered "There's a Ford in Your Future" (made by Gentile) $20.00

Glass, flat, with view of and advertising resort hotel $3.75

Glass, in shape of water faucet inside glass ball, advertising medicine and lettered "Turn off excess gastric acid, Nacton" $20.00

Lead, 3½ inches diameter with Dutch boy embossed on top, advertising paints $7.50

Steel, painted gold, 3 inches long, advertising cash registers $15.00

Steel, 3½ inches long, advertising tailors' trimmings $7.50

White metal, painted gold, 3 inches long, advertising typewriters $15.00

White metal, 3 inches long, advertising cheese $10.00

White metal, with illustration of Indian on one side, 2¾ inches long, advertising whiskey $7.50

White metal, in shape of shoe heel, 2½ inches long, advertising rubber heels $9.00

THERMOMETERS

Advertising, tin, 10¼×18 inches, depiction of man trying to ring bell with hammer, advertising beer $10.50

Advertising, tin, 5¾×13½ inches, with embossed package of cigarettes $5.00

Advertising, tin, 5¾×13½ inches, with embossed bottle, advertising soft drink $5.00

Advertising, tin, 2½×7¾ inches, advertising oil company $4.00

Advertising, tin, 3×8 inches, rounded ends, advertising Coca-Cola $15.00

Advertising, tin, in shape of bottle, 16½ inches long, advertising Nu Grape $8.50

Advertising, tin, with enameled illustration of girl with bottle, 27 inches long, advertising Pepsi-Cola $16.50

Advertising, tin, 15¾ inches long, advertising Moxie $15.00

Novelty, tin, in shape of standing Negro baby $12.50

Novelty, tin, 40 inches long by 8 inches wide, in shape of mail pouch $17.50

Novelty, tin in white metal frame with figure of chick at base $15.00

MIRRORS

Advertising shoes, with depiction of Buster Brown and Tige $25.00

Advertising malted milk, with depiction of woman and cow $16.25

Advertising pianos, lettered $8.50

Advertising women's shoes, lettered $10.00

Advertising cut tobacco, with depiction of dog $10.00

Advertising coffee, lettered $12.00

Advertising insurance, with depiction of mother and child $12.50

Advertising varnishes, with depiction of can of varnish $6.00

Advertising labor union, with depiction of boot $7.25

Advertising union suits, with depiction of cat $6.50

Advertising telephone company, with depiction of shield $12.00

Advertising food products, lettered $5.50

TRAYS

Change, advertising beer, Kansas City Breweries $19.50

Change, advertising hams, Cudahy Puritan $10.00

Change, advertising soap, Fairy $23.00

Change, advertising cigars, Garcia Grande $10.00

Change, advertising malt, King's Puremalt $24.50

Serving, advertising beer, Arnolt-Schaffer Brewery, illustration of woman and roses $32.50

Serving, advertising beer, Buffalo Brewery, illustration of woman's bust $45.00

Serving, advertising beer, Diehl, illustration of semi-nude $28.00

Serving, advertising beer, German Brewing Company, illustration of dogs with steins and smoking cigars $40.00

Serving, advertising soft drink, Moxie, illustration of girl $50.00

Serving, advertising bread, illustration of Gay Nineties girl $35.00

Serving, advertising carbonated beverages, illustration of horse and colt at stable $35.00

Placards, 1925 to 1929, advertising ammunition, illustrated, lot of five $31.00

Placard, celluloid, advertising cigars, illustrated with Indian girl in color $17.50

Placard, advertising gunpowder, illustrated with woman with dog $25.00

Placard, advertising cigars, illustrated with woman in bonnet and dated 1904, chromolithographed $85.00

Placard, advertising whiskey and gin, illustration of horse and buggy $5.00

Placard, advertising ginger ale, no illustration but lettered $3.50

Placard, advertising root beer, illustration of bottle $8.00

Poster, 12×14 inches, advertising lye, illustrated $5.00

Poster, roll-down type, 20×28 inches, advertising sarsaparilla, illustrated with bearded man and bottle $18.00

Poster, advertising soda, 11×14 inches, illustration of girl $20.00

Poster, advertising soda, 15×25 inches, illustrated with photographic reproduction of actress $35.00

Poster, advertising soda, 18×32 inches, lithograph by Tom Kelly of red-haired woman $35.00

Poster, advertising pharmaceutical firm, 7×19 inches, lettered on canvas $6.00

Print, advertising soap, 16×18 inches, framed, portrait of Negro child $40.00

Print, advertising soap, framed, portrait of girl on canvas $35.00

Print, advertising whiskey, 30½×36½ inches, framed and dated 1895, dogs playing poker, after painting by Coolidge $50.00

Print, advertising seeds and dated 1872, framed, 24×20 inches, illustration of thirty flower blooms $25.00

Print, advertising whiskey, 24×20 inches, framed, portrait of Negro man with horse and jug $45.00

Sign, metal, advertising milk, 15×22 inches, illustration of cow in floral sunburst $30.00

Sign, metal, advertising insurance, 30×39 inches, illustration in color dated 1912 $55.00

Sign, metal, advertising cigars, 5×8 inches, in shape of directional signal dated 1888 $20.00

Sign, metal, advertising beer, 25×37 inches, illustration of woman focusing light beam on bottles, dated 1907 $175.00

Sign, metal, advertising cigars, 10×14 inches, illustrated with box of cigars, ca. 1910 $16.00

Sign, metal, 9×13 inches, lettered, no illustration, ca. 1920 $5.00

Sign, metal, advertising shoes, 13×16 inches, illustrated with goose, ca. 1930 $6.00

Sign, metal, advertising cigarettes, 14×12 inches, illustration of bellhop with cigarettes $20.00

Sign, metal, advertising gunsmith, in shape of early rifle, 39 inches long $250.00

Sign, metal, advertising dyes, 22×17 inches, illustration of woman's life cycle $35.00

DISPLAY ITEMS

Cardboard stand-up figure of attractive girl, 4 feet high, advertising soft drink $135.00

Composition female figure modeling corset, small, advertising corsets $35.00

Metal chewing tobacco wall dispenser, 12 inches high, advertising tobacco $26.00

Porcelain display case, advertising cleaning compound, *ca.* 1920 $65.00

Wooden display horse, advertising harness, made by Toledo Display Horse Company $1,000.00

AMBROTYPES AND OTHER CIVIL WAR PHOTOGRAPHS

ALTHOUGH FINE DAGUERREOTYPE CASES have been collected for several years, thousands of examples of the photographic art of an earlier day now lie dormant, constituting a category of collectible sleepers with a bright future and probably an excellent investment potential. Among these are scenes taken during the Civil War and depictions of soldiers, Union and Confederate. That war, now removed from the youngsters of today by more than a century, has taken on a sudden fascination.

Actually, such examples of the photographic art in general, such as ambrotypes and tintypes, have been relatively neglected up to now except by dedicated institutions and a few students of the photographic art. Tintypes in particular may sometimes be encountered at giveaway prices. Quite recent books on the daguerreotype (invented in the 1830s by L. J. M. Daguerre and Nicéphore Niépce) have served to drive prices of good examples of this art up from the low levels of a very few years ago.

But daguerreotypes of Civil War scenes and soldiers are destined to rise in price within the next few years in the judgment of seasoned dealers, who, of course, make the prediction willingly when they have examples in stock. Mathew Brady was the outstanding Civil War photographer.

Ambrotypes (photographs on glass made by a process invented last century by James Ambrose Cutting) and tintypes (also called ferrotypes) represent almost untouched fields thus far with only some institutions and a bare handful of collectors seeking outstanding examples. But these and other examples of nineteenth-century photography will soon be eagerly sought by more collectors.

Also among the types of photographs just beginning to attract attention are the cartes de visite (calling card size photos of paper, measuring about $2\frac{1}{8}$ by $3\frac{1}{4}$ inches) introduced in the mid-nineteenth century. Many of these can now be picked up for a pittance.

We will not delve here into the history of photography, but I will point out that the lowly tintype deserves far more attention than it has so far been accorded. These photographs, which hastened the demise of the daguerreotype, were taken on sheets of tin or enameled iron that had been sensitized. The plates were made in various sizes, and several pictures could be taken on the larger ones. Tintype cameras were available for professional and amateur alike for a few dollars in the last quarter of the nineteenth century.

Both ambrotypes and tintypes were being made several years before the Civil War, and many of these were made during the war.

We tend to look upon the tintype as inconsequential and the result has been the loss of thousands of them to posterity. Tintype photographers once worked at fairs and carnivals, setting up shop in any space available. Photographers plopped their cameras on busy street corners in communities all over the country, inveigling passers-by to have their pictures taken for a dime. They were processed on the spot.

The important thing is that both the studios and the roving photographers of many years ago recorded not only war scenes but landmarks that have since been eradicated, buildings that have long since been demolished, homes that reflect the architectural styles of their periods, business establishments of a bygone era, Spanish-American War soldiers, battlefield scenes, famous personalities of the day, and even historic events. And these are the daguerreotypes, the ambrotypes, and the tintypes that will be most eagerly sought in the future and that will have the greatest value.

Pictures in handsome gutta-percha cases, signed by the maker or bearing the photographer's label, will fetch more than those not housed in cases, and an ambrotype or tintype encased in an attractive period frame will fetch more than unframed ones.

Floyd and Marion Rinhart have written a fascinating book called *American Daguerrian Art* (Clarkson N. Potter, Inc., 1967) and another devoted to the miniature daguerreotype cases, both of which will interest the collector of daguerreotypes. And they assembled a collection of more than a thousand daguerreotypes and six hundred ambrotypes, plus several hundred tintypes, cartes de visite, and miniature cases through diligent searching over a period of years.

Mr. and Mrs. Rinhart point out in an article in *The Antiques Journal* of July 1969 that the molded thermoplastic miniature picture case in which the finest daguerreotypes are found housed was invented by Samuel Peck of New Haven, Connecticut, and that their production began at the Scoville Manufacturing Company, Waterbury, Connecticut, in the 1850s. Peck's plastic compound, they say, is different from the natural plastic substance obtained from the gutta-percha tree.

Another major producer of cases was Edward Anthony of New York City.

The majority of early cases were made of wood covered by thin leather, and the inside of the cases, opposite the picture, usually contained a plush pad of satin, velvet, or silk. Cases made of thermoplastics are called Union cases.

Of more value than the plain cases are those interestingly or ornately decorated by die engraving, many of the designs, according to the Rinharts, being copies from old lithographs, paintings, sculpture, and books. There are also papier-mâché cases with mother-of-pearl inlays. Patriotic-design cases are in demand, particularly those bearing the likenesses of such figures as George Washington or adorned with flags, eagles, and cannons. Many of these were produced during the Civil War. Cases with daguerreotypes of Civil War soldiers are already fetching prices well above those for cases with unidentified men, women, or children.

The majority of cases now available measure about 2¾×3¼ inches, and are referred to as "sixth size" cases. These housed the smallest of six sizes of daguerreotypes, the largest of which measured 6½×8½ inches.

The collector will find that asking prices of daguerreotypes, ambrotypes, and tintypes will vary greatly right now. They are occasionally advertised for sale in the collector periodicals and, from time to time, will be found in some shops handling antiques. No doubt many are preserved, though most likely forgotten, in attic storage trunks.

I know one fellow who bought a large lot of early tintypes for a trifle a few years ago and thought so little of them that he glued them on Christmas cards with the message "Have an old-fashioned Christmas." I understand he is now going over his Christmas mailing list with the intention of trying to get them back!

Some recent prices follow:

AMBROTYPES

Beekman Hotel scene $75.00
Boy seated on fancy chair (oval) $16.00
Boy holding dog $18.50
Civil War soldiers $25.00 to 50.00
Elderly lady in white hood $17.00
Gentleman with cropped beard $15.00
Lady with fan $12.75
Post-mortem photo (rare) $35.00
Young man $12.00

DAGUERREOTYPES

Bearded man on sixth plate; flower basket embossed case $12.00
Bearded man in vest on sixth plate; floral embossed case $13.00
Boy in plain case $9.00

Boy on sixth plate, dated 1848, worn case $10.00

Boy, very young, ornately decorated case $16.50

Civil War soldiers, Union or Confederate $20.00 to 60.00

Cross-eyed young man, signed "Hawkins, Artist in Daguerreotype," sixth plate, case with sunburst motif $27.50

Elopement scene on sixth plate, gutta-percha case $18.00

Four-picture case, plastic, with three pictures, floral case $60.00

Funeral-altar-decorated case with 6×9-inch photo $8.00

Gutta-percha case, sixth size, with floral decoration $15.00

Gutta-percha case, sixth size, with deer and cupids $24.50

J. Gurney-signed case, $6\times4\frac{3}{4}$ inches, portrait of woman $25.00

Man and woman in two-picture case of gutta-percha $19.00

Man, with mirror in opposite side of case, gutta-percha $12.00

Mother and child in double case, leather $11.50

Pouting girl in gutta-percha case, sixth size $19.00

TINTYPES

Baseball player $13.00

Boy with dog $5.00 to 7.50

Boy with musket and long pole $15.75

Boys with milk can $14.00

Brigadier General Nathaniel Lyon, mounted in gold case $22.00

Child, in frame $5.00

Dog $4.75

Early automobile $8.00

Man riding pig $5.00

Miscellaneous unframed group ($6\frac{1}{2}\times8\frac{1}{2}$ inches), each $5.00

Miscellaneous portraits, 1870–1890s. Group of thirty $85.00

Miscellaneous unframed group ($4\times2\frac{1}{2}$ inches), each $.50

Soldier, Civil War $5.75 to 35.00

Animated clocks of early twentieth century. "Negus" is shown at upper left and children with swan and duck at top right. In center is the "Acrobat" or "Turner," and below are girls with mandolin and fan.

ANIMATED
AND TRAVEL CLOCKS
AND A FEW WATCHES

THROUGH THE CENTURIES since time began, there have been many ways of telling it, but among the most pleasant are some we will discuss in this chapter.

Not everyone can afford a pendant watch with a rock-crystal case surrounded by gilded brass or an eighteenth-century long-case clock and certainly not many timepieces by Holland's Christian Huygens or England's Thomas Tompion. But many of us can still afford a nineteenth- or early twentieth-century animated clock, or even less expensive early-day traveling clocks, figure clocks, or novelty watches of more recent date.

The animated clocks are now being sought, it's true, and prices are on the rise, but quite a number of them are still around. Animated or mechanical motion clocks were turned out in considerable diversity during the latter part of the last century. Although the majority of them encountered in this country apparently were made by American clockmakers, quite a number were also produced in Germany and several elsewhere. Even though a few seem to have been manufactured a bit earlier, their heyday began in the 1880s and continued into the twentieth century.

The majority of these clocks had dials which featured some type of animated action. Some were more complex than others but most were relatively simple, consisting of a single type of movement. Their original sales appeal was based on the animation itself; the clock works usually were simple and inexpensive, as were the round cases. Unquestionably many were simply discarded when they managed to get out of order; others were stashed away in basements or attics, and these are the best places to look for them.

Usually there was some type of figure (or a part of a figure, sometimes only a bust) depicted on the dial or face of the clock, a part or parts of which were activated by a mechanism. Most of the clocks were of the alarm type, too.

"The Mandolin Alarm" is a typical example. A woman in a loose-fitting garment holding a mandolin is depicted on the dial. When the mechanism was activated, her right hand strummed the mandolin strings.

"The Acrobat," made in Germany, features the moving figure of an acrobat on the top half on a 14½-inch-high case with the dial below. The figure performed various stunts for a three-hour period with a single winding.

Another German clock, this one with the animation below the dial, features a representation of a fountain. With a single winding, it offered an excellent imitation of water flowing from a fountain that lasted five hours. Both this clock and the one described above were offered by American wholesalers during World War I with a note to the effect that they would not actually be available until after the war.

The "Sambo" clock, also of foreign make, depicted on the dial a figure of a Negro woman who fanned herself and rocked a cradle with her foot when the mechanism was activated. This one wholesaled for only $2.50 in 1915. "The Negress" bears the head of a Negro woman, clad in a bandanna. When activated, the figure's eyes moved.

Another acrobat is featured on the dial of an alarm clock called "Turner." This one also performed gymnastic feats every few seconds when in action. It wholesaled in 1915 for $3.25.

The "Blinking Owl" is a clock of cast metal in the form of an owl with the dial in the figure's middle. When the clock was operating, the owl's eyes moved.

Clock with Western Clock Company movement housed in gold-plated cast-metal figural owl case, 8 inches high, ca. 1907.

This one stands 7 inches high, has a silver-plated case, and wholesaled in about 1914 for only $4.40. There were numerous variations of the moving- or blinking-eye clocks.

A group of clocks, each with animated figures on the dial, was made in Germany about 1913. One features a swan and a duck, another a shoemaker, a third a blacksmith, and a fourth a rocking cradle. These all retailed for under $5.00 and were equipped with one-day clock movements. Those depicting the smithy working at his anvil and the shoemaker at his bench are especially intriguing.

Clocks were made featuring woodchoppers, banjo players, flirting ladies with fans, and tobacco-chewing figures.

For some years after World War I, interest in animated clocks diminished, but it was reawakened during the thirties, and several animated clocks were made by Lux and others. They depicted such activity, when in action, as boys shining shoes, drinkers hoisting schooners of beer, windmills revolving, spinning wheels spinning, and church bells ringing. Many of these were alarm clocks. During the 1940s animated clocks with the likenesses of cartoon, comic book, and theatrical characters became quite popular, but these have been written about before and have reached rather frightening price levels already so that there is no point in including them in a book that is concerned primarily with less pensive sleepers.

Novelty figural clocks have been around for a long time and are far more available than the animated ones. Thousands were made of cast metal, and the majority were inexpensive when first produced.

One of the most delightful of these was marketed by Western Clock Company. It was in the form of an 11-inch-high cast-metal owl with a gold-plated case and a 3-inch-diameter dial. It came equipped with a 32-hour movement, and its wholesale price in 1907 was just $2.50. It was similar to the "Blinking Owl" described above but was not animated.

Novelty clocks with cast ornaments were made by the carload, but the collector may want to specialize in those clocks actually made in figural form. These have been crafted over a large part of the world and for many decades, but the easily accessible and less expensive ones date from about 1890 to around 1915—although during the jumping thirties a number that are of interest, though by no means valuable, were produced.

The New Haven Clock Company, early in this century, turned out a delightful one in the form of a chariot drawn by two birds and with a cherub atop it driving. This one stands 9 inches high and has a porcelain dial only 2 inches in diameter. It was available with either a one- or an eight-day movement. The retail prices were about $15 to $20.

Various cast figures holding the clock cases aloft were made in the early 1900s. One of the major producers of the cases was Ansonia. These timepiece

Early twentieth-century figural clocks. Top left: gold finish, made by Ansonia. Top right: gold-plated New Haven clock. From left on bottom row: "J. B. Ormolu" commercial Art Nouveau clock; snail clock by Ansonia; Art Nouveau clock by Ansonia.

Atlases were frequently winged cherubs or cupids but some clocks in the commercial Art Nouveau style substituted sinuous and occasionally buxom females to support the weight of the clock cases. Ansonia made one novelty in the form of a snail with a cupid astride it and its shell holding the clock case. This appeared in 1918 trade catalogues with a wholesale price of $5.00.

One of the most charming of all the Ansonia Clock Company's figurals was made in the 1890s in the shape of a dresser with eight elf-like figures clambering over it. The dial has an antique brass finish and measures 6¾ inches high. The clock was given the name "Fairies," but the figures bear a remarkable resemblance to those created by the artist Palmer Cox.

Ansonia also designed a clock in the form of an oven, on top of which was a frying pan held by a cast-metal figure. This one was called "Chef." One named "Myra" is actually a mirror in an ornate brass frame with the small clock itself housed in the lower part of the glass. Another Ansonia collector's delight is a clock in the form of a large fan being spread out by a small child. This came in either a silver or gold finish and a one-day time movement at a wholesale price, in 1898, of only $8.25. Its value today is several hundred per cent higher.

A clock in the form of a metal jewel casket, the movement being held in the center of a curved handle at the top, was made in the 1920s. The box had a removable lid and could be used for jewelry.

The M. S. Benedict Manufacturing Company of East Syracuse, New York, turned out in metal a group of clocks influenced by commercial Art Nouveau that would be considered perfectly horrible by the connoisseur but which will nevertheless hold an appeal for the collector. Several of these portrayed languid female figures in long garments reflecting the sinuous lines of the movement, either supporting the clock or supported by it. Most of them were given the so-called Venetian bronze or gold finishes.

The traveling alarm clock, contrary to widely held opinion, is no recent innovation: it goes back to the early nineteenth century, and it possesses both enough age and enough interest to be collectible.

Some were fitted into leather cases with carrying handles so they could be transported easily. Western Clock Company made a number of this type as did Seth Thomas. Waltham, a bit later, made rather similar travel clocks that folded into their leather cases when not in use, the cases being equipped with a snap lock.

In the 1920s the Hebdomas eight-day traveling clocks that folded into highly colored leather cases were popular but fairly high in price for the time, selling at $20 to $40. These dials and cases were oval, square, and octagonal, and the tooled leather cases gave them a swank appearance.

The less expensive clocks usually had one-day or 32-hour movements, and many could be bought for well under $10. In addition to the leather cases, there were also some embossed metal cases, and a few appeared in copper cases. Some of the metal cases were given gold finishes. In addition to the domestic traveling clocks, some made abroad, particularly in France, were offered in this country.

Watch out, too, for traveling watches, housed in folding cases similar to the clocks and available in this country prior to World War I.

There is also likely to be interest in novelty figural lapel and wrist watches. Clinton manufactured several about three or four decades ago, including one in the shape of a "Jitterbug" and bracelet watches in the form of snakes. New Haven made a lapel watch in the shape of a watering pot that originally sold for less than $2.00!

Not many of the clocks and watches described in this chapter have been offered for sale recently in the open market, but an animated clock in the shape of a Negro's head with a derby hat and movable eyes, made by Lux in the twenties, has been offered at $60.

A somewhat similar one called "Dixie Boy"—a figure with a necktie that swings back and forth as a pendulum—will bring $80 or more.

A French bronze figural clock featuring a musketeer with sword and cape on an onyx base and with an eight-day movement and strike is valued at $125. An animated dial clock with cast figures of Washington, Lincoln, and Franklin D. Roosevelt and marked "Steersmen of U.S.A." is valued at about $85.

The figural clocks will be found in a general price range of about $60 to $150, depending upon how ornate they are, the quality of their works, and their age.

Twentieth-century travel clocks should be valued at $12.50 to $50 or so, also depending on age and quality. The animated clocks in fine condition will bring more but will likely climb higher in value within the next few years than the other types described.

MUSICAL GADGETS

MUSIC BOXES, cylinder and disc, are of almost universal appeal to all who have an ear for music, but their prices have been rising during the past dozen years. Fine early ones—particularly boxes with interchangeable cylinders and featuring such miscellaneous accouterments as bells—will often cost more than $1,000. This removes them from the price range of collectible objects discussed in this book.

But still available at prices that are relatively low are many musical objects in the gadget category (though the current prices are almost certain to ascend because of the increasing popularity of mechanically transmitted music in general). Foremost among these are musical albums, whose heyday was sixty to eighty years ago, when a favorite hobby of young ladies was making a scrap book: pasting photographs of relatives, friends, neighbors, and miscellaneous celebrities in photograph albums.

Many of the albums were elaborate affairs with embossed leather or decorated velour covers, gilded page edges, and brass or gilt corners and clasps. Albums in general enjoyed a wide sale in the late nineteenth and early twentieth centuries. Many are on the collectors' market today, usually at low prices, since there are not too many people who get a thrill from looking at photographs of someone else's kinfolk of a century ago. Nevertheless, many of these ordinary albums are interesting, and readers who would like to know more about their background will find an informative chapter devoted to them in Katharine Morrison McClinton's *Antiques of American Childhood* (Clarkson N. Potter, Inc., 1969).

We are not concerned here, however, with routine albums but with those equipped with musical units, which played a tune when the album was opened. Though it may surprise many, such albums were being sold in the very early years of this century at less than $5.00. The First National Co-operative Society's Cash Buyers Union, a pioneer discount organization established in Chicago in 1885, displayed in its 1905 catalogue a flat music album equipped with a two-air music box at only $3.25. The album itself had a decorated celluloid cover with a fancy oval mirror in a frame. The album had space for thirty small photographs plus six post-card-size photos.

The musical units with which the albums were fitted were quite simple and inexpensive, similar to the one- and two-tune mechanisms fitted into the little round or oblong music boxes of the same period that sold for $5.00 to $15 and were not really in the same class with their grown-up counterparts. Even so, the musical albums are pleasant—and entertaining—examples of the objects that amused our ancestors, and they are well worth preserving if the mechanisms are still operable.

You'll find these albums in a number of antiques shops, many priced at $45 to $125.00. This is certainly a far cry from their original selling prices, but as they become more scarce, watch for values to go still higher.

Miniature musical units have been fitted for many years into literally dozens of objects ranging from canes to snuff boxes. The early ones are frequently of considerable value, not so much from the incorporation of the musical unit in them but from the fact that the objects themselves were made of costly substances, some set with jewels, so that we will not include these high-priced artifacts here.

On the other hand, there are on the market a great many more recent objects in which music-playing units were incorporated, and some are still being made. Seeking these far less expensive articles can be a great deal of fun, and every indication is that they will yield you a profit if held for several years.

Most of these things are in the category of novelties. They became fads when first introduced. Sales zoomed, then eventually declined as different types of novelties emerged from the drawing boards to catch the popular fancy. As a result, many of them have been consigned to storage in the attic, along with yesterday's bonnets, dresses, and costume jewelry. There are dolls, trinket boxes, and a large miscellany of other small boxes, many produced early in this century, though their popularity has continued over a period of decades since. There have been musical long-case clocks for years, but our grandfathers could also buy musical alarm clocks for around $10. The clocks were made atop bases that contained quite small musical units.

Individuals interested in the broad field of music boxes should know that an organization of dedicated collectors exists called the Musical Box Society International. Those who collect music boxes of any kind can learn a great deal about them through membership in such an organization. Such a wide diversity of articles with musical mechanisms have been made that surprises will await the amateur who decides to venture into this area of collecting.

Objects whose musical units have been damaged may present a problem. There are still some artisans who can repair the musical units, but, in the case of inexpensive gadgets, the cost of repair may exceed the value of the item.

The values of musical albums and other novelties will depend upon their construction, their age and rarity, the condition of their mechanisms, and the type and quality of the musical unit. Here are prices of some miscellaneous units, including a few older and more costly ones together with some recent ones:

Album, *ca.* 1890, two-tune unit, French movement $45.00
Album, Victorian, 14×12×4½ inches high, celluloid cover, brass corners
   $77.50
Album, Victorian, with original pictures intact $79.00
Book box on stand, 4½×4×1½ inches high, pull-up lid, silver finish $45.00
Clock, 6 inches tall, brass and glass case, key-wind, one tune $55.00
Clock, German, 6 inches tall, German eight-day movement, plays on hour,
   handle on top $60.00
Clock, carriage $90.00
Clock, 14 inches long across base, 4½-inch-diameter dial, four-tune musical unit
   plays on half hour, old $175.00
Charm, mosaic top, 1×¾ inch, with gold pin, Swiss movement, recent $25.00
Chest, miniature, copper, wood-lined, 10×6×3 inches high, three-tune Swiss
   musical movement, 1912 $85.00
Chest, miniature, mahogany, 10½×6×7 inches high, English, brass handle,
   with two-tune unit $52.50
Chest, miniature, brass trimmed, oriental, two-tune unit $65.00
Doghouse, miniature, 8×5×7 inches, metal dog figure, two tunes $70.00
Jewel box, gilded medal, 5×3×3 inches, velvet-lined, two tunes $37.50
Lighter, table, India, 8 inches high, Evans lighter, one tune $19.50
Print under glass frame with musical unit at base, 12×9½ inches $49.50
Singing birds, depending on age $35.00+

ATOMIZERS AND SMELLING-SALTS BOTTLES

THE USE OF PERFUMES dates back literally to the Garden of Eden. Containers for perfumes survive from ancient Egypt, Greece, and Rome, but the bulb atomizer that reduces the liquid scent to a fine spray is of much more recent vintage. So is the smelling-salts bottle, the other item we will discuss in this chapter.

They emerged in numbers in the nineteenth century when the toilet-water and cosmetics industry came of age, and quickly evolved into decorative objects for milady's chambers. Both atomizers and smelling-salts bottles have become

Bohemian atomizer of cut glass at left and "Mary Gregory" type with enameled figure at right were offered by Bloomingdale's of New York City in 1892 at $1.69 and $1.19, respectively.

collectible objects today; those bearing the mark of master craftsmen in glass have attained a state of eminence that endears them to the status seeker. Into this category fall bottles produced by René Lalique and his son Marc in France and those made at the Steuben Glass Works under the sternly guiding hand of the late Frederick Carder.

But there are hundreds of other scent bottles and atomizers and those delightful little vials called smelling-salts bottles that have been crafted in glass since late last century that are definitely worth seeking.

The manufacture of atomizers and scent bottles in general has, in many instances, approached the stature of a fine art. This development was inevitable since to house sweet fragrance in abominable packages is unthinkable, even though from time to time it has been both thought of and done.

Atomizers have been made in almost every conceivable type of glass and in almost every conceivable shape. "Mary Gregory" atomizers with delicate enameled figures of children have been produced both in this country and abroad. So have "Bohemian glass" atomizers with patterns or designs cut from one casing of glass to another. Sparkling atomizers have been created in cut glass of the "Brilliant period" (1880–1915). Nor were these handy little containers ignored by the designers of "art glass": they will be found made of such exotic glasses as "Peach Blow," Baccarat's "Amberina Swirl," Victor Durand's art wares, satin, and others, and they have been designed by such artists in cameo glass as Emile Gallé and the Muller brothers.

And yet, the fascinating atomizer has been largely ignored by most of the experts who have written books about glass in recent years and who have been preoccupied with grander pieces such as bowls, candlesticks, centerpieces, and vases.

The smelling-salts bottles were around in some quantity as this century dawned, and the majority that are still encountered are made of either cut glass or pressed glass designed in imitation of cut. These small vials, a great many of which were fitted with hinged tops of sterling or plated silver, were intended to hold pungent substances, a whiff of which helped enable ladies of earlier years recover from the fainting spells, real or imaginary, to which so many frail ladies of an earlier generation seem to have been susceptible.

Smelling-salts bottles were American-made derivatives of what the Europeans variously termed vinaigrettes, pomanders, and pouncet boxes. The European varieties, usually in boxlike form, date back at least to the eighteenth century and came in handy for ladies who, traveling not only the countryside but also some of the city streets, found themselves assailed by offensive odors, since in those days garbage pickups were not routine and those who had garbage to dispose of found the public byways a handy place in which to dump it.

Originally, the vinaigrette was a silver box with a perforated lid in which was enclosed a sponge or spongelike substance that had been soaked in a pungent

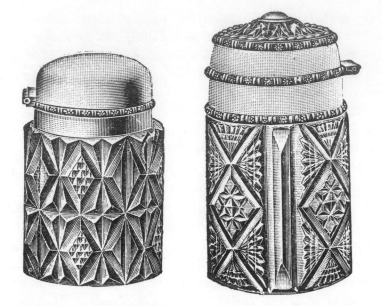

Smelling-salts bottles of cut glass, ca. *1900*.

liquid such as vinegar. But in the United States the word was used to describe an odd-shaped bottle utilized to hold liquids of a scented nature. A typical vinaigrette of the late nineteenth century in this country was a sort of scimitar shape, and these were fashioned in cut and pressed glass, both of which are desirable.

There were also many triangular-shaped vinaigrette bottles with a base much narrower than the mouth. These were closed by a stopper and a hinged cap that fitted around a metal collar on the bottle's neck. The most desirable ones had tops into which were set stones, precious or semi-precious.

Similar were so-called odor bottles, an early twentieth-century designation for perfume bottles. Another name widely used at the outset of the century was simply "scent" bottle. Some of the early odor bottles came in plush-lined cases and were sold in jewelry stores and other high-class mercantile establishments.

As compared with the top-quality atomizers and allied bottles made by Lalique, Gallé, Tiffany, and other famous glassmakers and designers of the nineteenth and early twentieth centuries, the novelty versions that sprang from the assembly lines in subsequent decades of this century are trivial, but it should be remembered that today the collectors of trivia outnumber the collectors of fine antiques by at least 100 to one and that the prices of nostalgic trivia have shown fantastic increases in the past few years. The unmoneyed collector will probably not be able to amass a very large collection of art-glass atomizers and smelling-salts bottles. But he can, if he sets out now before the stampede, garner a varied batch of the more recent vials that can provide him with a delightfully cluttered den without having to dip into much more than his grocery budget.

Highly collectible scent and "vinaigrette" bottles ca. *1900. Two at top are of cut glass; one at bottom right, also cut glass, has jeweled top.*

Here are some typical current prices that include both the inexpensive and the more costly varieties of atomizers and allied bottles:

Atomizer, 3 inches tall, heavy cut crystal $5.00
Atomizer, 6 inches tall, Baccarat "Amberina Swirl" $35.00
Atomizer, 5¼ inches tall, sterling overlay on clear glass $24.00
Atomizer, 5 inches tall, etched amber to clear "Bohemian glass" $35.00
Atomizer, 5 inches tall, clear crystal glass, gold-plated fittings $6.00
Atomizer, 8 inches tall, clear crystal (Holmspray cologne) $4.50

Atomizer, DeVilbiss, light blue vine on dark blue ground by Durand $75.00

Atomizer, Steuben Rosaline glass $70.00

Atomizer, cameo by Gallé, three acid cuttings $175.00

Atomizer, cameo by Muller Freres $97.50

Atomizer, cameo by Richard, signed $115.00

Atomizer, "Wave Crest" glass, swirled body, enameled florals $90.00

Atomizer, cut glass with silver-plated trimmings by Meriden Britannia Company, 5-ounce capacity $35.00

Atomizer, 7 inches high, crackle glass, *ca.* 1928 $9.00

Cologne bottle, Baccarat "Amberina Swirl," clear bottom $38.00

Cologne bottle, ruby "Bohemian glass," Vintage pattern $35.00

Cologne bottle, frosted glass with beehive top, *ca.* 1934 $3.50

Cologne bottle, "Miss Boston," 1-dram bottle in hardwood case $5.50

Cologne bottle, 7-ounce decanter-shaped crystal glass, "Eau de Cologne" $4.00

Cologne bottle, cut glass, signed Hawkes $50.00

Perfume bottle, cut glass, 6 inches tall, clear button cane pattern $65.00

Perfume bottle, flask-shaped enameled glass, 2 inches tall $14.00

Perfume bottle, crystal with silver overlay, 4 inches tall $14.50

Perfume bottle, Amberina glass, "Thumbprint" pattern $45.00

Perfume bottle, Baccarat "Amberina Swirl," steeple stopper $35.00

Perfume bottle, 4 inches tall, camphor glass $3.00

Perfume bottle, 4⅝ inches tall, enameled cranberry glass $35.00

Perfume bottle, seahorse-shaped in porcelain, crown stopper $10.00

Perfume bottle, cut glass, "Harvard" pattern, sterling top $28.00

Perfume bottle, Fry Foval glass with red stopper $95.00

Perfume bottle by Lalique, 6½ inches tall, prism shoulders and sides, frosted shell stopper $22.50

Perfume bottle by Moser, 5 inches tall, swirl-ribbed, heart-shaped stopper $40.00

Before the Avon figural bottle collector starts screaming that she has been ignored, let us point out that these bottles experienced a rather meteoric rise in values for a few years as Avon bottle collecting became a hot fad, but that many collectors became disenchanted with the company's earlier policy of reissuing the same designs from time to time and that some prices are now declining. In addition, there are several books available that deal exclusively with the Avons.

EARLY AUTOMOBILE
AND AVIATION
"LITERATURE"

THINGS JUST HAVEN'T BEEN THE SAME since those whizzing products of man's genius outmoded the noble horse as a means of transportation. We get where we're going faster these days—when we do get there, but the luxurious and leisurely pace of the horse-and-buggy days is a joy of which the modern generation has been deprived, thanks to the automobile, the train, and the airplane.

But even these vehicles are no longer spring chickens as modes of transportation, and they are likely to be outmoded one day by spacecraft of one type or another that will enable us to get where we're going even faster—and more precariously, if that's possible.

Antique automobiles and their accessories have been collected for years, the former by the affluent and the latter by those with lighter purses. For those who simply cannot afford the classic and vintage cars themselves, the field of early printed materials relative to them can be a highly lucrative area of collecting, because early automobile "literature" is disappearing rapidly and prices are already climbing the ladder. (Those interested in automobile accessories of the thirties will find a chapter devoted to them in my book *Collecting Nostalgia*.)

In the category of automobile printed materials that will be increasingly sought at rising prices are manufacturers' sales brochures, operating instruction manuals, advertising circulars, shop manuals, flyers distributed by franchised dealers, lithographed posters depicting early models, trade cards illustrating cars manufactured before 1935, salesroom display cards, early photographs of cars, and, in particular, catalogues of automobile supplies and accessories.

There has been a demand for several of those classifications for some years but it is currently expanding, and since the supply is limited this pressure exerts a strong influence on values. Prices still vary widely, the earliest illustrated items bringing fancy prices. A 1912 Maxwell Motor Car catalogue was recently offered for $27.50, which may seem a fairly steep price, but the truth is that this is only a portent of what is to come.

Automotive supply catalogues are currently in great demand, especially on the part of collectors and restorers of those magnificent early cars. Restorers also avidly seek shop manuals, which provide specific instructions relative to matters involved with restoration and repairs.

One of the most dedicated collectors of automobile salesroom catalogues in the country is Edwin L. Chandler of Doraville, Georgia, a commercial artist. Al-

Automobile catalogues from the collection of Ed Chandler of Doraville, Georgia. Some scarce catalogues are worth $150 to $200.

though Mr. Chandler's collection is by no means the largest in the country (one collector in Philadelphia has amassed more than 12,000 of them!), it is composed of more than five hundred choice catalogues, some of them dating back to about the turn of the century and now extremely rare. Mr. Chandler began collecting these catalogues in the 1930s while he was still a youngster in Newnan, Georgia. He not only obtained them from automobile dealers but frequently from manufacturers of cars as well. After several years of collecting, he had piled up about two hundred catalogues. He neglected his collecting for some years but began again a few years ago.

Indicating the value of some of the choice and scarce catalogues is the fact that Mr. Chandler paid as much as $150 each for a few of them and has paid around $100 each for others, although the bulk will probably fall within the $25–$45 price range.

For about twenty years Mr. Chandler was a designer for the John H. Harland Company, well-known commercial printers of Atlanta. He had a natural knack for drawing from childhood, he says, but also subsequently studied art. Now he has turned his erstwhile hobby into a profession. He is the author and artist of *Antique Car Coloring Book Number 1* (E. L. Chandler Company, Inc., Doraville, Georgia), and did drawings that are faithful representations of early cars for a 1975 calendar. The coloring book contains fifteen full-page drawings of early autos ranging from a 1908 Franklin Landaulet and a 1915 Ford Coupé to a 1931 Austin two-place roadster, plus a descriptive text that reveals his intimacy with the early-day vehicles.

The catalogues and brochures most eagerly sought today are those that deal with automobiles no longer made and many of whose names are not familiar to the younger generation, such as the Winton, Stutz, Reeves, Mitchell, Gardner, Locomobile, and dozens of others, and those relating to classic cars of the thirties.

Because vehicle designs change so frequently and often so radically over the years, recent printed materials about them will soon be fetching what will seem to the noncollector high prices, but some may be picked up now for just a few dollars.

A few years ago this material was being abundantly advertised for sale in such collector advertising periodicals as *The Antique Trader*. Now most ads in these publications are placed by collectors wanting to buy them. There are, however, numerous specialized publications in the antique automobile field itself that carry advertisements of printed matter for sale. In addition, catalogues, brochures, posters, and sales manuals may be encountered at the larger flea markets, and there are a few specialist dealers.

It may be interesting to note in passing that a passion seems to be developing at this time for early chauffeur badges and marble gear-shift knobs. Carl Rustine of Route 3, Stroudsburg, Pennsylvania, is an avid collector of chauffeur badges, and C. R. Maize of Somerset, Pennsylvania, actually collects cast-iron toys but deals extensively in chauffeur badges, gear-shift knobs, and other adjuncts associated with early automobiles.

The recent feats of spacecraft, about which we will have more to say later in this book, have served to stimulate an interest in all aeronautical things, including the early planes themselves, although there are not many collectors who have personal hangars in which to accommodate these. However, an interest is developing in the early crop dusters, which helped work a revolution in American agriculture, and literature about the pioneer crop-dusting planes as well as parts of the planes themselves, including propellers, tails, and insignia, together with instruments, appear headed for something of a collecting boom among aviation enthusiasts.

It is of special interest that Delta Air Lines, which now ranks among the nation's largest commercial air lines, had its beginnings as the world's first crop-dusting service; and if the boll weevil had not migrated from Mexico in the early 1900s to devastate Dixie's cotton fields, there might never have been a Delta Air Lines. Another pioneer airline, Chicago & Southern Air Lines, became part of Delta through a merger in 1953. Expansion has continued to the present day, and the company is restoring and preserving some of its original duster planes, which saw their first service in Macon, Georgia. Anything relating to the beginnings of these two companies—and other pioneer airlines—is now eagerly sought. These include early timetables, which are now worth several dollars each. Typical is a 1928 Northwest Airways timetable offered at $4.00. Collectors also seek early tickets, airline counter placards and insignia, and all types of printed materials, including early issues of the *Aircraft Year Book* and documents and photographs of the pioneer planes. Books dealing with the beginnings of the airline industry and with pioneer feats in the air are now beginning to move upward in price. Various editions of *Aircraft Year Book* will bring $7.50 to as much as $25 for the 1920 edition. Magazines in the field of aircraft are worth $3.00 and up.

A horse-drawn model of an old Portage Railroad passenger car measuring 31½ inches in length was bid in for $1,000 in March 1972 in a unique sale in auction annals. This was a sale of railroad relics, artifacts, and rare and historic documents belonging to the Pennsylvania Railroad Museum. The sale was conducted on the South Concourse at the Thirtieth Street Station in Philadelphia by Samuel T. Freeman and Company, and consisted of almost two thousand lots. The two-day sale attracted throngs far beyond expectations and even standing room in the large roped-off area in which the sale was conducted was at a premium.

Bidding throughout the two days was spirited, and veteran auctiongoers said many prices could only be described as "fantastic." For example, two albums of assorted photographs of locomotives brought $300. A scrapbook of about four

Model of 1834 Old Portage Railroad passenger car measures only 31½ inches long. It was sold in 1972 for $1,000. Photo courtesy Samuel T. Freeman & Company, Philadelphia.

hundred railroad and building passes fetched an astonishing $600. A collection of photographs of locomotives typical of each class in 1868 made $650. Another album of assorted photographs and prints of steam locomotives and tenders cost the buyer $200. The catalogue *Standard Locomotive Cars of the Pennsylvania Railroad Co.*, 1876, plus some loose photographs, fetched $600. An album of twenty-seven photographs of Pennsylvania Railroad scenery was bid in for $275, and another similar album brought $350.

Susquehanna Railroad scrip, consisting of a little over 1,100 pieces for $100, went to the highest bidder for an almost incredible $3,200, and $1,000 was paid for a brass locomotive plaque labeled "Norris Locomotive Works, Lancaster, Penna., No. 68. John A. Durgin Constructor." Two thousand dollars was shelled out for a wheel from the locomotive "John Bull"; $1,400 was paid for some assorted books of stock certificates and a photostat sheet; and $500 was the price for a copy of *Traveler's Official Railway Guide, 1873–75.*

Prices paid for printed materials in particular were consistently high, and would certainly surprise those who are unaware of the mounting interest in early materials pertaining to this mode of transportation. A group of assorted plans and diagrams made $650; a batch of employee passes was sold for $230; six Pennsylvania Railroad schedules fetched $250; and an 1880 railroad poster in full color was sold for $350. Moreover, both an illustrated brochure distributed by the auctioneers in advance of the sale and the actual sale catalogue have already become collectors' items.

Although numerous mementos related to railroading, ranging from dining-car silver and china to conductors' punches, are being currently collected, with silver and china making a strong surge, early railroad watches are now sleepers (even though there are some dedicated collectors of them), and little has been written about them. Such watches with cases decorated with engravings of locomotives and railroad cars will soon be in prime demand, say experienced dealers, due to some extent to the fact that this mode of passenger transportation as we once knew it seems on the way out.

The railroad watches were manufactured in large numbers between the 1880s and 1915. Among the numerous manufacturers making them were the Dueber-Hampden Watch Works, Illinois Watch Case Company, Jas. Boss, Elgin, Cresent Watch Company, Crown, Joseph Fahys, and others. The original selling prices varied greatly, according to the precision of the works and the metal of which the cases were made. For example, gold-filled cases were bringing around $20 wholesale in 1900, but watches with so-called silveroid and ore-silver cases were wholesaling for as little as $2.20. The zealous collector can assemble a magnificent collection of railroad watches alone, each with a different view of a locomotive on the case. (Most locomotives, incidentally, were depicted with smoke belching from their stacks, the early trains being among the chief contributors to air pollution.)

Since the wrist watch has outmoded the pocket watch, more collectors are turning these days to the old pocket watches in general, and the cases with railroad scenes constitute an interesting specialized area. Some of the watches illustrated in this chapter indicate the variety in which they were produced.

Railroad equipment catalogues issued last century and early in the present one, railroad bonds, and souvenir booklets and brochures picturing either early equipment or scenery along early routes are all destined to increase in value soon.

Frank Rochat, for three decades an employee of the Central Railroad of New Jersey, is one of the country's most dedicated collectors of everything pertaining to early railroads, and he sits today in his home in Carlstadt, New Jersey, surrounded by trains and early railroad memorabilia. Not by dozens or scores or hundreds of them but by more than a thousand. For trains have taken over a large part of Frank Rochat's life. From his easy chair he can view simultaneously a century-old steam train, a Jersey Central "Blue Comet," an endless array of freight cars, an equally endless stream of passenger cars, dining cars, cabooses, and, in fact, almost every type of rolling stock that for well over a century traversed the terrain of America.

These are "toy" trains, hundreds modeled after their full-grown counterparts, and today they constitute Frank Rochat's avocation and his vocation. Mr. Rochat, now in his sixties, began work as a yardman for the Central of New Jersey and subsequently worked in almost every capacity from conductor to fireman. Trains became as much a part of his life as breathing, eating, and sleeping. By a decade ago, he had assembled more than 1,200 pieces of rolling stock in miniature, supplemented by hundreds of accessories. His trains ranged from tiny replicas to such "monsters" as a foot-high and 24-inch-long "Buddy L" engine. When a piece of equipment broke down, he repaired it himself. Today, he not only collects but also repairs and sells model trains, which right now are becoming sizzling items on the collector's market.

Mr. Rochat is typical of thousands whose vocation has led to a hobby intimately associated with their means of earning a living. Many other individuals who have become extremely knowledgeable about their own areas of collecting have also turned their hobbies into income-producing ventures in their retirement years.

Here are some prices currently being asked for types of objects described in this chapter:

AUTOMOBILE LITERATURE

Brochure, Dort, 4 pp., 1913 $10.00
Brochure, Durant, illustrating six 1928 models in color $9.00
Brochure, Hupmobile, 1928, color illustrations $15.00
Brochure, Nash, 1928, color illustrations $12.50
Brochure, Western Auto Supply, late 1920s $3.50
Brochure, Willys-Knight, 1927 $10.00
Catalogue, Autocar Motor Trucks, 1920, 80 pp. $11.00
Catalogue, Buick sales, 1920, 30 pp. $20.00
Catalogue, Excelsior Auto Supply, 1904, 64 pp. $25.00
Catalogue, Ford sales, 1921, 16 pp. $17.50
Catalogue, Manufacturers Supplies, Philadelphia, 1915, 222 pp. $13.00
Catalogue, Maxwell Motor Car sales, 1912 $27.50
Catalogue, Metz Touring Car sales, 1915 $20.00
Catalogue, Sears, Roebuck auto supplement, 1920 $6.50
Circular, Chevrolet advertising, 1922, 12×21 inches $7.50
Circular, advertising 1910 Columbian, 8×10 inches $7.50
Instruction books, various, 1920s and 1930s, each $7.50 to 25.00
Magazine, *American Automobile Digest,* 1920 issues, each $5.00
Magazine, *Motor Talk,* 1905 issues, each $7.50 to 10.00
Operators' manuals, 1930s and 1940s each $7.50 to 10.00
Operators' manuals, 1914 to 1925, each $12.50 to 22.00
Shop manuals, Chevrolet, 1930s, each $15.00
Shop manuals, Studebaker, 1930s, each $9.00 to 12.50

AIR TRAVEL

Aircraft Yearbook, various editions, 1920 to 1942, each $7.50 to 25.00
Magazine, *Aircraft Journal,* 1919 issues with aircraft covers, each $10.00

Magazine, *Air Service Journal,* 1919 issues with aircraft covers, each $4.50

Magazine, *The Ace: Aviation Magazine of the West,* 1919 issues, each $4.00

Magazine, *Model Flying,* 1933 issues, each $3.50

Magazine, *Popular Aviation,* 1930 issues, each $5.00

Magazine, *Sportsman Aviation & Model Flying,* 1933 issues $3.50

Maintenance book, Hispano-Suiza Aeronautical Engines Model A-I-E Wright-Martin Aircraft Corp., 1918 $50.00

Maintenance book, *Aeroplane Construction, Operation and Maintenance,* by Johnny B. Rathbun, 1929 $15.00

Maintenance book, *Modern Aviation Engines,* by Major Victor W. Page, 1929 $20.00

Page Nicholas Beazley Airplane Company catalogue, 90 pp., 1931 $15.00

RAILROADS

Bonds, early railroads, various, each $5.00 to 35.00

Booklet, souvenir of the Royal Scot Railroad, Chicago, 1933 $3.50

Breakfast menu, Western Pacific Railroad $1.50

Brochure, Chicago, Milwaukee, St. Paul and Pacific, 1935 $3.50

Brochure, Chicago and Northwestern Railroad, 1904 $4.00

Dividend checks, California Street Cable Railroad Company, 1895, each $3.50

Engineer's report, Green Bay, Milwaukee & Chicago, 1852 $20.00

Luncheon menu for group excursion, Southern Pacific, 1939 $1.00

Map, folding, of California, issued by Southern Pacific Railroad and showing rail lines in state, 1925 $3.50

New Haven Railroad book of rules $5.00

Timetables, miscellaneous, pre-1930, each $2.00 to 20.00

Travel brochure, Northern Pacific, 1917 $1.50

Travel brochure, Northwestern Pacific, *Vacation 1927* $2.50

Travel brochure, Southern Pacific, *Oregon Outdoors,* 1930s $1.50

Watches with pictorial cases, each $40.00 to 150.00

Waybills, nineteenth century, each $1.50 to 5.00

NAPKIN RINGS, NAPKIN MARKERS, AND FOOD PUSHERS

SCORES OF INDIVIDUALS are addicted to figural napkin rings, hundreds or perhaps thousands to souvenir spoons, but who is addicted to nonfigural napkin rings and markers or those unquestionably utilitarian devices known as food pushers? Yet in their own way these objects are as fascinating as dozens of other things dating in the same period and now being collected with great passion.

There are numerous mementos of earlier years intimately associated with babies that are being preserved and treasured, and among these are baby spoons and mugs, especially those charming "Franklin Maxim" mugs that are decorated with the observations of the multitalented author of *Poor Richard's Almanac*. But for an uncrowded field one may wish to turn to the silver and plated napkin rings that yielded helpful service in the years before the paper napkin took over the home as well as the restaurant.

The reign of the napkin ring extended roughly from the 1880s until World War I. The figural ones have been written about time and again, but the nonfigural ring has been largely ignored and does indeed constitute a sleeper, as those who have seen them will likely agree.

A variety of sterling-silver rings enriched by openwork designs, chasing, and engraving were being turned out by this country's silver manufacturers in 1900. The decorations veered from Baroque to Rococo, and a little later commercial Art Nouveau. These were priced according to weight, and merchandise catalogues of 1900 show them at wholesale prices of $2.00 to $10.00.

Silver-plated rings were much cheaper, some selling wholesale for as little as $1.75 per dozen although the more ornate and larger ones were priced as high as $16.25 a dozen.

There were plain sterling napkin rings with no decoration other than perhaps beaded edges; some boasted decoration that covered most of the exterior surface; and others had openwork or cut-out designs. Plated rings were engraved with floral designs primarily but occasionally also with such things as sheaves of wheat,

Turn-of-the-century silver-plated napkin rings. Top row from left: heavy embossed finish; embossed center with burnished shield; satin, bright-cut, beaded border. Center row: satin, bright-engraved; satin, hand-engraved; satin, bright-cut, Rococo border. Bottom: Art Nouveau decor; satin, hand-engraved, beaded border; satin, hand-engraved, gold-lined.

cupids, birds, and berries. Many rings were engraved with names of their owners; others were lettered "Mother," "Father," and "Baby." The rings were offered both individually and in pairs in boxed sets. Among the major manufacturers of the plated rings were E. G. Webster & Son, Barbour Silver Plate Company, and Homan Silver Plate Company.

Those of sterling silver, of course, possess an intrinsic value, but collecting even those of plated silver holds a promise of reward in fun and profit. Sterling rings that have become tarnished can be brightened with a good silver polish, but there is nothing to do with the plated ones whose silver coat has worn off except to have them replated.

The contents of older homes occupied by the same residents over a period of several decades will often yield napkin rings, because it has not been that long since their use was discontinued. Sterling ones will be found in some antiques shops, but not many, due largely to the current preoccupation with the figural variety.

The food pusher, too, has largely gone out of fashion, but these were once widely used for pushing food scattered about a platter into a centralized area from which it could be served more easily. They were also used to push food on baby's plate into a location from which it could be scooped up in those delightful crooked-handled spoons that babies used without quite so much danger of its being pushed onto the tablecloth instead by youngsters whose aim was not quite mature.

The food pusher consists of a handle to which is attached an oblong flat metal piece somewhat resembling a miniature crumb scraper. Since it was a piece of special-usage tableware, it was customarily sold individually rather than as an integral part of flatware sets, though they were available in many flatware patterns. Some were sold, however, boxed with a baby spoon, the patterns of each piece matching.

Although the majority of the food pushers seem to have been made of plated silver, some sterling ones were turned out. One encounters these articles with some frequency in catalogues issued early in this century, but their appearance diminishes with the ensuing years. Just as is the case with many other articles of special-purpose tableware once used but now outmoded, the food pushers are fairly scarce. Food and nutrition habits have changed, and today's children are not required to eat every scrap of food on their plates so it seems unlikely that the pusher will be revived. This, coupled with scarcity, means that prices for these little table articles are likely to be good once they are "rediscovered" by the collecting fraternity.

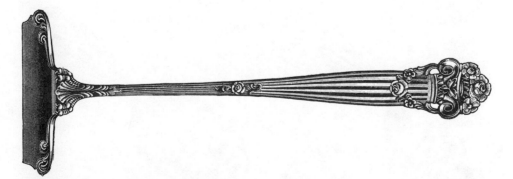

Sterling-silver food pusher of 1900 with gilt bottom originally wholesaled for $3.00.

47

And this brings us to napkin markers, holders, and clips. The markers, much simpler contrivances than the figural napkin rings, were made of sterling silver in varied designs and with a flat surface upon which one's names or initials could be engraved. The engraving shields were sometimes beaded or otherwise decorated. Pierced designs predominated, taking the form of leaves, vines, and the like.

Some napkin markers were also made of plated silver, and these retailed just prior to World War I for only about a dollar. E. G. Webster & Son designed many of the more interesting napkin clips, whose name derived from the fact that they actually held the folded cloth napkin in a rather flexible grip so that the cloth square could be easily inserted and extracted.

As differentiated from the clips, napkin holders were narrow oval rings with bases extended outward into feet so that they could be placed upright on the table. Their metal bands were much narrower than those of the conventional napkin rings that we discussed earlier in this chapter. Some are appealing because of their decoration and, like the other articles mentioned above, are quite small so that space for housing a collection will prove no problem.

So few of any of these objects have been pursued by collectors thus far that it would be pointless to attempt to compile values for them. The only advertisement that I've noticed for napkin clips within the past year was for a pair of silver-

Sterling-silver baby spoons of 1900 depicting animals and nursery rhyme scenes.

plated ones by James Tufts. The clasps of these were decorated with mice, and the price asked was a rather astonishing $90. But there are undoubtedly other simpler ones around that can be bought for just a few dollars.

Nonfigural napkin rings of plated silver, food pushers, and markers and holders also should be available for under $10; those of sterling will come higher.

Before leaving this field it should be pointed out that the delightfully decorated "crooked handle" baby spoons themselves and the bib holders used to attach the napkin securely around baby's neck and frequently made with figural clips are being collected, but neither of these categories has as yet been adequately explored and sleepers may still be found in both.

MESH AND BEADED BAGS

IF YOU KEEP SOMETHING LONG ENOUGH, it's bound to come back into style, and mesh or beaded purses are no exception. They've been in and out of fashion more frequently than ankle-length dresses, and they may be back in by the time you read this since they already are being brought out of hiding and placed on the block.

Mesh bags were fashionable in the late 1800s; they were in style as this century began, and they have reappeared and disappeared at intervals since. And in case the reader thinks *all* mesh and beaded bags and purses have been consigned to oblivion, let her take note of the eminent Sotheby Parke Bernet Galleries sale in May 1972, where mesh bags were snapped up by wealthy purchasers:

A gold-mesh change purse from the thirties (a period in which the mesh and beaded purses and bags returned to great popularity) brought $160. True, it was set with small rubies and diamonds. A 14-karat gold-mesh evening bag set with two cabochon sapphires and graced by a tassel of seed pearls fetched $200. If you think that price high, read on. A gold-mesh evening purse set with six diamonds and with a cabochon sapphire thumbpiece made $400—the same sum paid for an Art Deco-style gold- and platinum-mesh purse with a diamond set clasp and a cabochon sapphire thumbpiece. Still another Art Deco two-color gold- and platinum-mesh purse with a diamond-set clasp and jade thumbpiece was bid in at $50 more.

Happily for those who were unable to attend this sale and purchase one of those choice mesh bags, there are others now being ferreted out of trunks and the backs of dresser drawers and offered for sale, most at prices considerably lower than those cited above. The majority of the mesh and beaded bags and purses just starting into the antiques marketplace were far less expensive to start with, not being set with precious stones, and consequently can be bought for a comparatively low price.

In the 1890s mesh purses of woven wire with silver, rolled gold, or gilded tops and necks of meshed metal bars that opened and closed in the manner of accordion hat racks were being offered as the latest fashion. Most of these were small, and attached to them were a chain and a ring by which they could be fastened to chatelaines, also fashionable then. But there were also mesh hand purses with traditional snap tops. These sold, complete with chains, at prices from about $5.00 to $25.

As the twentieth century dawned, sterling-silver mesh-type purses and shopping bags fashioned of soldered links were being offered. Although some of the smaller purses could be acquired for an outlay of around $10, those of "shopping-

Chain-mesh bags with sterling-silver links, ca. 1900.

bag" size (ranging up to 6½×4¼ inches) were tagged at $12.50 to as much as $75 or $80.

These were known then as "chain purses and shopping bags," and similar ones, a good bit cheaper, were made of plated silver.

About the time of the outbreak of World War I in Europe, fine-mesh metal bags were evident everywhere. Those of sterling were high in price and thus limited in production, but those of German (nickel) silver abounded. Square shapes predominated but there were some in cathedral dome shape. One type was referred to by manufacturers as made of "goldine" metal: these were gold-plated, and one could buy a large size one for $15 to $20. Some were given

"Mandalian" enameled-mesh bags (top row) and French steel-beaded bags (below) came into style in the 1930s.

52

a platinum finish "fish-scale" mesh, which was a very close mesh; others featured an open-ring mesh and still others were crafted in what was then called a "fine baby mesh."

Some bags had silver and others, silver-plated frames; some bore gold trimmings. Nearly all were equipped with a snap closure and carrying chain. Some of the frames were hand-engraved or embossed with flowers, scrolls, or geometric designs. A few draw-string-type ring-mesh purses also appeared at this time, one pictured in a 1915 catalogue of Otto Young & Company of Chicago being offered at a wholesale price of just $1.75. It was of German silver.

Some new designs in mesh bags appeared around 1918, featuring fringed bottoms or tassels, but they were generally of the same basic type as had appeared earlier. The gate tops were also back in style again, and a very small purse of linked rings that could be carried concealed in the palm of a glove made its advent. Incidentally, too, nickel silver self-opening gate tops for mounting handmade beaded bags were offered separately at three or four dollars.

Colorful enameled mesh bags became stylish in the 1930s, a diversity of designs being created by using colored enamels. These included alternating stripes of color, flowers, and birds that were particularly popular with the younger set. Naturally there was a "Bird of Paradise" design. The enameled-mesh purses vied in popularity with sleek leather ones and clutch bags of calfskin or simulated leather.

Guess what was back in style again in the forties? Bronze-finished mesh bags with cloisonné tops. These were fitted with mirror, rouge, and loose face powder. And gold-finished and silver-finished bags that were almost exact duplicates of those being offered in 1900 were also back on the store shelves again.

The offerings just being made of the mesh and beaded bags of earlier years have been in a price range of $5.00 to $35 except for the outstanding examples tendered at the Sotheby Parke Bernet sale. They are beginning to crop up now at outdoor flea markets with indications that those selling them dug them out of their mother's or grandmother's erstwhile treasures.

They do constitute a new category of collectibles, and you can watch for prices to go higher before long. Any in first-class condition that can be found at $5.00 to $10.00 could be bargains.

MINIATURE BOOKS

THERE'S A LAND-OFFICE BUSINESS in comic books under way. Would you believe $300 for a copy of *Action No. 3,* a comic book of 1938 featuring the characters Superman and Zatara? Or $145 for the 1940 *Detective No. 36,* delineating the adventures of Batman? Those prices are by no means exceptional for comic books in which well-known fictional characters made their first or an early appearance. So unless you want to invest a lot of money, you'd better turn to other types of "literature" to collect.

Miniature books fascinate many. The earliest of these actually appeared not long after the invention of printing and are exceedingly scarce and costly; but others have been published far more recently and are finding a good many addicts. Some are beautifully printed and handsomely bound, and some titles were published in limited editions, which tends to push their values up. There came from the press of William Edwin Rudge, for example, an edition of a New York telephone directory that measured 4¾×6¼ inches.

Many businesses have issued miniature books as souvenirs of anniversaries and special occasions, and these, much less expensive, can nevertheless provide the basis for a challenging collection.

Collectors differ as to how small a book must be to be properly classified as a miniature. Some suggest books with pages a maximum of 4 inches high; others insist that books larger than 2½ inches are not true miniatures. Nevertheless, there are now large numbers of collectors who seek books measuring 4 to 4½ inches high.

The Book of the Queen's Dolls' House Library, edited by E. V. Lucas, was published in England in 1924 in a limited two-volume edition and is devoted entirely to the miniature library and paintings in the world-famous doll palace made for Queen Mary on display at Windsor Castle. The two volumes are devoted entirely to the description of miniatures.

All types of books have been published in miniature editions, including almanacs, Bibles, picture books, and religious tracts. Some are bound in hard covers, some in soft covers. The late President Kennedy's inaugural address was published in a book of 32 pages that measured only $2\frac{5}{8} \times 1\frac{7}{8}$ inches in size. Bound in calf and stamped in gold, it was selling a decade ago at $3.50 but its value has since risen.

Miniature books continue today to come off the presses, private and public, and all are collectible. Outstanding among recent publishers of the tiny books were the Black Cat Press of Norman Forgue in Chicago and the press of Achille J. St. Onge in Worcester, Massachusetts. Collectors who do not insist on rare and lavishly bound limited editions can assemble a good library of miniature books for a relatively small sum.

If you grew up in the twenties you may remember a series of miniature paperback books called Little Blue Books. These began their career as a series of reprints, largely of the classics and sometimes in abridged form. This project was the brainchild of E. Haldeman-Julius, author, agnostic, and publisher, and by 1940 he had published nearly two thousand titles.

The Little Blue Books originally sold for a nickel, and, later, when somewhat thicker books were added, the price was a dime. Haldeman-Julius reprinted everything from the plays of Shakespeare to nineteenth-century classics and then began issuing some original books written especially for the series. They included a group of what might be called antireligious tracts and also a group about sex, some of which purported to tell young men what every young man ought to know and young girls what every young girl ought to know, and some even told adults some things they could have got along very well without knowing.

The Little Blue Books were widely advertised, especially by mail, from Haldeman-Julius' headquarters in Girard, Kansas, and undoubtedly millions of copies were printed. Probably few persons indeed ever thought that one day some of these books might be collected and would sell for substantially more than their original prices, but that day is arriving right now. A mid-1972 catalogue of one of the country's most respected antiquarian book dealers lists several Little Blue Books issued in the 1920s at $2.50 each. These include one written by Jack London entitled *An Odyssey of the North,* published in 1920. Haldeman-Julius also published an anti-Catholic propaganda magazine called *The Debunker* in 1929–30. Issues are worth about $1.50 each.

Another series was the Big Little Books. There are presently a number of collectors of these, but prices are still in the $4.50 to $20 range. How long they will hold there is anybody's guess, and some experts are guessing it will not be long. As Herman C. Carter pointed out in an article in *Collector's World,* Whitman did not reprint old titles so that, in effect, every Big Little Book is a first edition.

These books were born in the thirties or late twenties (opinions differ), offspring of Whitman Publishing Company. However, Big Little Books is currently

Some of the original Big and Better Little Books, published by Whitman Publishing Company in the 1920s. Photo by Herman C. Carter, Tulsa, Oklahoma.

a registered trademark of Western Publishing Company, Inc. The books measured about 3½×4½ inches in size, appeared in stiff cardboard covers, and at one time more than five hundred titles were available. Subject matter ranged from illustrated stories of comic strip characters to both biographical and fictional treatment of movie stars and real-life heroes.

Most collectors now seek the books dealing with the well-known strip or radio serial characters so these prices are relatively high. But there are other volumes in this series that deal with lesser-known characters, such as Barney Baxter, Zip Saunders, Dan Dunn, Speed Douglas, Pal Nelson, Eric Noble, et al., and one will discover that these can often be found at prices lower than those asked for the titles dealing with better-known characters.

Some books in the series featured flip pages with the cartoon characters appearing in the top corners giving the illusion of animation when the pages were flipped rapidly.

Several titles were added to the series in 1950 and others just a few years ago. A companion series, Better Little Books, by the same publisher, is also collectible. These began appearing in the late thirties.

Collectors of the Little Blue Books and the other series mentioned are no different from dedicated collectors of rare books: they want their acquisitions to be in good to fine condition with no torn pages, damage to the covers, or defacements—so forget about damaged copies.

Although, as noted, the majority of titles will fall within the $4.50–$20 price range, some can be found for as little as a couple of dollars and scarce ones are tagged at around $40; but within the next year or two, the $40 figure may be exceeded and only a few may remain at under $4.50.

The prices that follow represent a cross-section of those being currently asked, except that no scarce or rare volumes are included in the miscellaneous miniatures:

BIG LITTLE BOOKS

Alley Oop and Dinny $12.50
Apple Mary and Denny Foil the Swindlers $10.00
Buck Rogers, various titles $15.00 to 30.00
Captain Midnight, various titles $6.00 to 15.00
Dick Tracy, various titles $8.00 to 30.00
Donald Duck Headed for Trouble $10.00
Flash Gordon and the Power Men of Longo $15.00
Flash Gordon and the Witch Queen of Mongo $25.00
Gene Autry, various titles $3.50 to 20.00
G-Man on Crime Trail $4.00
Green Hornet Strikes $10.00
Green Hornet Cracks Down $10.00
Jim Craig, State Trooper $6.50
Joe Palooka, the Heavyweight Boxing Champ $25.00
Little Miss Muffett $16.00
Little Orphan Annie, various titles $4.00 to 35.00
Mickey Mouse and the Bat Bandit $13.00
Mickey Mouse and Pluto the Racer $12.00
Phantom and the Sign of the Skull $6.50 to 10.00
Popeye Sees the Sea $5.50 to 7.00
Red Barry $4.00
Red Ryder, various titles $3.50 to 12.00
Roy Rogers, various titles $3.50 to 12.00
Tarzan, various titles $8.00 to 25.00

Tom Mix, various titles $4.50 to 15.00
Two-Gun Montana $4.00

The Bible in Miniature for Children, Boston, *ca.* 1965–70 $8.00

Daily Manna, Troy, N.Y., *ca.* 1850 $10.00

Dew-Drops, New York, *ca.* 1850 $7.50

Fanny's Picnic, by "Aunt Fanny," Buffalo, N.Y., 1866 $10.00

The Fullness of Christ. From the Remarks of W. Romaine and Others. Millbury, Mass. $15.00

History of the Bible (woodcut illustrations), Troy, N.Y., 1823 $20.00

The Lighthouse-Keeper's Daughter, Boston, *ca.* 1855 $8.00

The Little Treasure, Containing a Kind Word for All, Philadelphia, *ca.* 1861 $8.50

Miniature Almanack for the Year of Our Lord 1824, Boston, 1823 $10.00

Philip Hamilton, The Soldier's Ordeal, or Virtue's Reward, by D.M.B., Philadelphia, 1865 $8.50

Story of the Grimalkin Family, by "Aunt Laura," Buffalo, N.Y., 1863 $8.50

The Thumb Bible, by J. Taylor (a reprint of an edition of 1693 published in London), New York, no date, boxed $12.50

DUG BOTTLES

BOTTLE COLLECTING is, and has been for the past several years, probably the most widespread hobby in the United States.

In recent years almost reams of books about bottles of every conceivable kind have poured from the presses, and they continue to come. Bottle "experts" have emerged overnight; bottle shows rival general antiques shows in number—and size. Bottle collecting knows no age limits, sex, color, or creed.

Taking advantage of the activity in the bottle field, several commercial firms a few years ago began issuing new figural bottles, a pioneer in the field being the James B. Beam Distilling Company, whose first figural bottle actually appeared in 1952. The company began issuing the figurals in series in 1953. Apparently they helped sell Jim Beam Whiskey, for through the years they have multiplied astonishingly.

Other companies followed suit, the major ones at the outset being distilleries. In recent years almost every conceivable type of business has been issuing figural bottles. The more they came, the more fantastic the shapes—and the higher the prices of the earlier ones rose.

Figural bottles honored everybody and everything, from President Eisenhower to the late Dr. Martin Luther King and from banks to cable cars. The price of one scarce bottle, issued in a limited edition of only 106 to help celebrate the centennial of the First National Bank of Chicago by Beam, reached the point that it was selling for more than $2,000! There were bottles made of glass and bottles made of ceramics.

Activity in the marketplaces became frantic. Both manufacturers and firms specializing in selling these brand-new bottles took full-page advertisements in the leading collector periodicals to vend their wares. And prices continued rising, in the opinion of some beyond reason.

Many felt the bubble had to burst, and apparently that is just what it is now doing. Prices of the new figural bottles have dropped, severely in many cases, and the advertisements have diminished sharply. The interest of collectors began to veer back toward the old standbys: historic flasks, early blown bottles, early whiskey and other spirits bottles, and the products of pioneer American glasshouses.

But there has now emerged a rugged breed of collectors: those who go out and dig their own bottles. Already their ranks are legion, and yet seasoned observers of this sphere of activity say that interest is really just awakening and that "dug" bottles represent the coming boom in collecting.

City folk and country dweller alike are doing the digging these days. They swarm out each weekend to city dumps and through the countryside, armed with shovels and paraphernalia, clad in old clothing, because bottle digging can be a mess. But it is also a tremendous amount of fun. Children are joining their parents in the fray, because in this venture there is something for everyone to do. The best places to dig, say those in the know, are around old garbage pits and at the sites of old outhouses, the latter being grandpa's favorite place for discarding his old spirits bottles. Almost every type of dug bottle is of interest: soft drink, sarsaparilla, patent medicine, other medicinals, ink, beer, whiskey, wine, rum and other spirits, food, and so on.

Most collectors of dug bottles specialize in one category; otherwise, their homes would be overrun by bottles. Diggers both collect and sell, keeping those in the category they have decided to collect and selling the others they encounter while digging.

The hobby can be dangerous. The novice is advised to heed the advice of the experienced digger, because the dangers range from possible cave-ins of earth to potential shotgun blasts from irate landowners whose property is being damaged without their consent.

If you're interested in digging bottles, you should be aware of the fact that, generally speaking, bottles dating from about the middle of the last century to the turn of the present one are of most interest to collectors. Also, for the most part, handmade bottles are of greater interest than those made by the automatic pressing machine, which was invented by Michael J. Owens and which was put into use shortly after this century began. To learn how bottles were made and how to distinguish a handmade bottle from one made by the automatic machine, the beginning collector should study one or more good books on this subject, such as *The Antique Bottle Collector* or *The Mouth-Blown Bottle,* both by Grace Kendrick or *The Illustrated Guide to Bottle Collecting* by Cecil Munsey.

The broad, general types of bottles most likely to be encountered today by diggers that are of interest to collectors include the following:

Spirits and soda bottles and flasks; medicine bottles, including bitters and patent medicines; mineral waters; ink (and even early glue bottles); food bottles, which contained everything from olive oil to pickles; snuffs; perfumes and cosmetics; and—the newest field of interest—fruit or canning jars and bottles.

I won't attempt to list prices here; to give a solid indication of values by types would be impossible, since to present a fair cross-section would require a large volume in itself, and several have recently been devoted to just this. Suffice it to say that prices will start as low as half a dollar and go up, but thousands are available from $.50 to about $10. The extremely scarce ones not likely to be encountered by the casual digger can fetch prices of $50 to several hundred dollars.

Early bitters bottles will range from $50 up, but later ones are available from $7.50 to $25. A few collectors specialize in poison bottles, most of which are priced between $3.00 and $15. Early mineral water bottles will fetch $20 to $100. Although scarce whiskey bottles are high, many are still available in a price range of $7.50 to $25. Medicine bottles are abundant at $1.00 to $10.00, though here again scarce ones are higher, and soda or soft drink bottles can be found priced at $5.00 to $25, rarer ones bringing up to about $65. And thousands of food containers can be bought for under $10.00.

The point of this very brief chapter is that "dug bottles" constitute the coming field for collectors in spite of the masses already involved and that as more and more bottles disappear from their burial spots in the soil into collectors' hands, the prices have only one way to go.

Those interested will find in the Selected Bibliography at the end of this volume several helpful books on this subject.

BOTTLE OPENERS, CORKSCREWS, AND BOTTLE CAPS

IF THE FIGURAL BANDWAGONS now rolling seem overcrowded—and many of them are—crank up a wagon of your own. Then start loading it with such appurtenances of the well-dressed kitchen (or bar area) as silver bottle openers and corkscrews and silver bottle caps, so many of which were made in figural shapes. And should you settle on this field, don't limit your acquisitions to figurals: novelty shapes and designs for these household and party necessities date back to the nineteenth century.

Silver bottle openers and corkscrews are by no means prosaic articles. Through the years they have been designed and produced in dozens of sizes and shapes, and they have constituted gracious adjuncts of the tightly capped or tightly corked bottle of spirits—or, if you prefer, liniment and gargling oil.

One could assemble a fascinating collection of folding silver corkscrews alone. The screws (which, of course, were not of silver but of iron or steel) folded into silver cases when not in use. Simple and relatively inexpensive ones were made that merely folded into the handle without benefit of case, but these are of lesser merit as collectors' items than those with their own cases.

Also, since attention is presently being focused upon pocket knives, the combination pocket knife-bottle-opener-corkscrew is likely to take on added value soon. Many of these with gold-front and gold-filled cases were being marketed in the 1920s at prices of $7.50 to $15.

There are combination bottle openers and corkscrews with sterling-silver handles delightfully decorated with chased designs, predominantly floral. Sterling-handled openers were manufactured by a number of silver companies in the last quarter of the nineteenth century and on into the twentieth. A sterling opener appeared about the time of World War I with an engraved scene depicting a dancer kicking a gentleman's top hat, the design including, for full measure, cards, poker chips, and a dice cup.

All kinds of novelty figural openers began appearing in the 1920s, and these

Unger Brothers bottle openers of sterling silver, ca. 1900.

included corkscrew combinations. Of far more interest, however, are tiny cork-screws appearing about the turn of this century with sterling-silver figural tops, some with Art Nouveau designs.

Eminently worthy of inclusion in any collection of bottle-opening accessories are figural corks, intended to replace the plain corks pulled from bottles of wine and other spirits. Among the most fascinating of these was a series made early in this century by Unger Brothers, manufacturing jewelers, silversmiths, and glass cutters of Newark, New Jersey. These corks were fitted with sterling-silver figural tops that were miniature replicas of clowns, jesters, dogs, and the like, or with round sterling tops with figures created in repoussé, some of these also in the Art Nouveau style so popular in this country and abroad late in the last century and

63

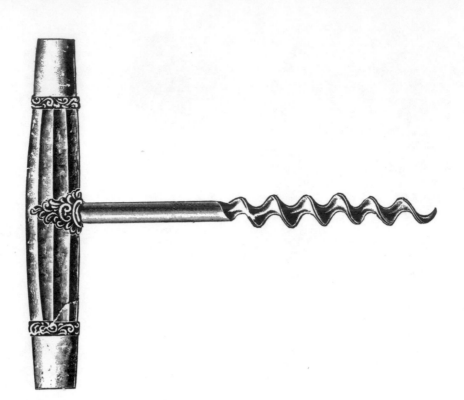

Silver-handled corkscrew from the early 1900s.

early in this one. Many other types of novelty figural corks have been made since, but none are quite equal to those of sterling by Unger.

Although we are concerned here primarily with the sterling objects, it should be pointed out that figural openers and corkscrews of other materials are also collectible and that those who pursue the types of advertising and promotional items discussed earlier will certainly be interested in the advertising openers and screws. These have been made for many decades in tremendous quantities, most of them having been given away by bottlers of soft drinks, distillers, and retail establishments selling soft drinks and spirits. These are still being produced, but earlier ones will bring $1.00 up.

We are listing below some prices not only for the sterling items but also for other miscellaneous ones, since there will be collectors interested in all types.

BOTTLE OPENERS

Advertising, brewery, 1906 $4.00
Advertising, Moxie, hand opener $1.00 to $2.50
Advertising, Moxie, combined with bottle stopper $2.50
Advertising ginger ale with the "White Rock Girl" depicted $5.00
Coca-Cola hand opener, brass $5.00
Coca-Cola wall opener, dated 1925 $5.00

Coca-Cola wall opener with sprite figure, *ca.* 1940s $3.00 to $5.00

Sterling-silver with Art Nouveau design $15.00

Sterling-silver, chased decorations, miscellaneous, early twentieth century $6.00
to $17.50

Sterling-silver, plain, late nineteenth or early twentieth century $6.00 to $15.00

CORKSCREWS

Advertising, Anheuser-Busch, bottle-shaped $4.00

Bullet-shaped, twentieth century $1.00

Combination screw, opener, and knife, gold-plated case $12.50

Combination screw and cap lifter, wood-sheathed, 1920s $7.00

"Old Drennon" promotional corkscrew $3.00

Staghorn-handled iron screw, 4½ inches long $5.00

Sterling-silver figural top, early twentieth century, small $9.00

Sterling-silver folding corkscrew with case $8.00 to $13.50

BOTTLE CORKS

Sterling-silver, figural or pictorial tops $7.50 to $15.00

BRUSHES, BRUSH HOLDERS, AND TRAVELING TOOTHBRUSH CASES

BRUSHES HAVE BEEN WRITTEN ABOUT BEFORE, but there are some with exquisitely decorated tops and handles made early in the present century that simply have to be discovered by collectors soon. Fine brush holders, too, are due for a spurt. And while it is not in precisely the same category, the traveling toothbrush holder of three quarters of a century ago is just beginning to attract some attention.

Hairbrushes with silver figural backs abounded in the early part of this century, among the choicest being those decorated in the Art Nouveau style. Several silver manufacturers made them, and we predict that they are destined soon for a period of popularity with the small sums for which a few have been offered within the past year or two rising sharply.

Those crafted with sterling handles in the form of languid females are delightful and put to shame those chaste and antiseptic handles and backs of brushes that now inhabit the retail shops. Among the leaders in turning out Art Nouveau hairbrushes was Unger Brothers, mentioned earlier. Some lovely brushes lie neglected on the shelves of antiques shops because their silver coat has become begrimed through the years and no one has taken the trouble to apply a coat of silver polish that would uncover the word "sterling."

There are many other hairbrushes still around with either sterling or silver-plated backs embossed with flowers and sinuous stems characteristic of the new style of the early twentieth century. Some were offered in the first decade of the century in boxed sets that also included a hand mirror and a comb.

A treasure for collectors would be an Unger Brothers sterling-back brush upon which was embossed the head of an Indian, replete with headdress. This was made early in this century as a part of this company's "Indian" pattern toilet set, which also included a variety of other articles necessary to milady's toilet. On the handle of this brush there is embossed a quiver of arrows flanked by

Unger Brothers figural-back hairbrush in Indian pattern, ca. *1900.*

tomahawks, the bottom part of the quiver being delineated in a sinuous Art Nouveau curve.

Garment brushes of various types, including the whisk and the "bonnet duster," were also made with embossed figural handles of sterling and plate and cry out to be collected. The once lowly whisk was converted by imaginative designers into a thing of grace and beauty by the addition of patterned sterling handles

Bonnet brush with sterling-silver handle by Unger Brothers.

and shafts. So, too, were the hat brush, the clothes brush, military brushes, shaving brushes, toothbrushes, and even crumb brushes! You wouldn't think that the toothbrush could ever be more than a starkly utilitarian object, but in the hands of turn-of-the-century designers it became an exciting thing. Those with sterling handles are surely around somewhere, waiting to serve, for one thing, as an inspiration to today's toothbrush-makers.

Novelty figural brushes and brush holders of all types were revived in the 1930s but few were fashioned of sterling even though many of them are intriguing.

Then there were the traveling toothbrush holders (utilized in the home as well as during travel) of glass and metal, including silver. The crystal holders of tubelike shape were capped by either silver or plated screw tops. Folding toothbrushes were available for folding into beautifully embossed silver cases. These can constitute a unique collection. In addition, there were combination tooth-

Toothbrush with silver handle by Unger Brothers, ca. 1900.

brushes and cases made as a single unit, the case serving as the handle when the brush was used. Some had hinged tops into which the brush itself was fitted after use.

Since collectors in general are not intimately familiar with these objects available to their forebears, their values for the time being are in a state of flux. The crystal toothbrush bottles are certainly worth a few dollars now, and they will be worth more when a fad for them is generated.

Hairbrushes with sterling backs and mounts have been selling occasionally for $25 and under. The figural ones should be worth considerably more, so now's the time to look for them.

The objects discussed in this chapter are destined to be collected tomorrow, and, as the Greeks once said, "Who knows aright of tomorrow's fortune?"

CAMEO JEWELRY, CHARMS, AND VEST-POCKET PICTURE FRAMES

THERE'S SOMETHING ABOUT A CAMEO that catches the eye of the dowager and the scullery maid alike. And now that Victorian jewelry is beginning to intrigue collectors who had looked down their noses at it earlier, it's time to examine some of the cameo jewelry, novelty charms, and vest-pocket picture frames that were showered in such abundance on our grandmothers.

Make no mistake about it: good Victorian jewelry—and quite a lot of it was good—is advancing rapidly among the collectible items of the past century, and prices are clambering upward with an almost frightening alacrity. Cameo jewelry —brooches, bracelets, stickpins, rings—has been in favor over many decades. Some of it is good, some mediocre, and some downright bad.

Cameos were carved in relief on shells, stones of various kinds, and particularly agate, glass, or other hard materials. Cameos have been fashioned from jewel stones, and some of these date back centuries, but these are beyond range of us mendicants, so we will be concerned here primarily with those carved from shells. Relatively simple—and therefore relatively inexpensive—ones were made in large quantities in the final quarter of the nineteenth century, and they have continued to be produced in the present one. The intricately carved cameos are substantially higher in price, because they required greater time and, frequently, considerable skill. The quality of many early twentieth-century cameos was extremely poor, the faces cut into the shell, coral, or stone degenerating into caricatures.

Color, according to Robert W. Miller, writing in the May 1969 issue of *The Antiques Journal* ("Admire Your Cameos—but Please Don't Call Them Art!"), is important to collectors. Maroon, he says, is a greatly treasured color, though those with nearly black ground are rarest. And rich pink is more desirable than pale pink.

Classical themes have been rather consistently favored by the cameo artists, and the classical head (brow circled with a laurel wreath or head encased in a helmet or a cowl) was used with greatest frequency. Rolled gold-plate rings with tiger-eye cameos were selling in the 1890s for as little as a couple of dollars and the so-called solid gold rings with tiger-eye cameos could be had for $7.50 to $20. There were also pink shell cameo pendants decorated with small diamonds and 10-karat gold chains in a $10.50–$28 wholesale range. Those willing to settle for similar pendants set with Baroque pearls instead of diamonds could buy them cheaper. Cameo brooches, gold-filled ones with pink shell cameos, retailed for as low as $5.00. There were numerous designs of mountings. In 1919, Marshall Field and Company offered "solid" gold cameo brooches at $9.00 to $36, the solid gold turning out to be 10-karat. The 14-karat gold mountings came higher, as much as $57 being asked for a choice one with seed pearls around the engraved border. The phrase "solid gold," incidentally, was used to differentiate the mountings of 9-karat or higher gold content from those that were merely gold-filled; pure gold is 24 karats. The popularity of the cameo at that time was summed up in this way in the Marshall Field catalogue:

Cameo on shell in twisted-gold frame, early 1900s.

"Cameos always are in fashion. This charming bit of art has maintained its general popularity since early Roman days. They are hand carved and consequently no two are exactly alike. Each cameo has a certain individuality. It is this distinction that gives the cameo its charm."

Ladies of World War I days were also wearing cameo lavalieres and festoons and cameo scarf pins in gold mountings. Nor did the male of the species neglect the cameo: he wore cameo rings and stickpins in his tie. Interest in this jewelry did not diminish after the war, and in 1926 *House Beautiful* devoted a long and profusely illustrated article to the crystal cameos of France, the finest of which are exceptionally costly.

Cameos will be found in virtually all of the antiques shops that handle jewelry, they are plentiful at antiques shows, and you are likely to find at least one among your grandmother's treasures. Good though not the finest quality cameo brooches of the 1850–1900 period can still be found at prices of $40 to $90; but if you're buying for investment, you should learn to distinguish good work from mediocre. Because of their unflagging popularity, the good ones are almost certain to increase in value in the years ahead. In the meantime, they can be worn for the admiration and envy of your friends.

Charms—those irresistible little trinkets worn on bracelets, chains, watch fobs, pins, and the like—have been manufactured in carload lots and in almost every design conceivable, and some inconceivable, for decades. They have been made of solid and rolled gold plate, of silver, of enamel, and other substances, and they have been set with semi-precious and precious stones. Hundreds of thousands were sold late in the last century at prices under a dollar, but thousands of others were considerably higher. The price is regulated by quality. Charms are available in the form of horses, musical instruments, weapons, locomotives, baseballs, anchors, hands, barrels, fish, anvils, ice tongs, acorns, turtles, boots, opera glasses, and grocers' scoops. They were made as miniature replicas of books, bulls, bicycles, elephants, magnifying glasses, mortars and pestles, monkey wrenches, thermometers, conductors' punches, checkerboards, and suitcases. It is their novelty that gives them their appeal, and particularly for teen-agers. Their fascination for the young—but not too young—is as strong today as it was a century ago.

Watch charms abounded before the wrist watch displaced the pocket watch. They were set with such stones as onyx, sapphires, pearls, garnets, diamonds, and bloodstones.

In a category by themselves are the emblem charms made for many fraternal and allied organizations such as the Masons, Knight Templars, Odd Fellows, Knights of Pythias, B. P. O. Elks, Junior Order, United American Mechanics, Independent Order of Foresters, and others. Many of these were quite costly, being set with precious stones and enameled, engraved, and otherwise decorated. These small charms can be great fun to collect. The trifles will never be of much more value than they are now, but the finer ones set with stones are likely to appreciate in value as long as people continue to wear jewelry and costume decorations, and that is likely to be a long time indeed.

The portable picture case is a less obvious collectible. Lockets have been around for generations, but the so-called vest-pocket picture frame constitutes a sleeper.

These frames appeared in some quantity in the first two decades of this century. Resembling the vanity case in appearance, they were small enough to be

Turn-of-the-century novelty charms in gold and rolled gold plate.

carried in a man's vest pocket but they were also frequently attached to the person by a chain. They consisted of a hinged case in which two pictures could be housed, and they were made of silver and of gold. Many featured a small plate on the exterior of the case on which the owner's name could be engraved. The finest of the gold cases were priced above $50 in 1918, but gold-filled frames could be bought from about $5.00 up. The adoption of informal attire and the diminishing popularity of the vest apparently had an impact upon the production of these vest-pocket picture frames, for one almost never encounters them in jewelry catalogues issued from 1930 on. Consequently, their relative scarcity may enhance their value.

Since these picture cases are rarely advertised, their price is a matter between buyer and seller, and charms are available in such a wide range of prices from a dollar up that it would be pointless to list values here. There follow, however, prices recently asked for cameos:

Brooch, carved head of girl, pink and white gold-filled oval frame, $1\frac{1}{2}\times1\frac{5}{8}$ inches $39.50

Brooch, carved female head in 14-karat yellow gold frame $85.00

Brooch, "Rebecca at the Well," gold frame $42.50

Brooch, carved oval shell, twisted-gold frame $40.00

Brooch, carved carnelian, silver frame $57.50

Brooch, carved bust, 10-karat gold frame set with small diamond $75.00

Brooch, carved classical figure with swan, 14-karat twisted-gold frame $80.00

Locket, white-on-black cameo, gold-filled frame $30.00

Ring, 10-karat gold with $\frac{1}{2}\times\frac{1}{2}$-inch cameo on pink shell $20.00

Ring, man's, 10-karat gold with small square cameo, warrior and maid $18.50

Ring, 14-karat gold, small cameo on pink shell $35.00

Slide chain, gold, 26 inches long, with $\frac{1}{4}$-inch diameter cameo $95.00

Stickpin, $\frac{1}{2}\times\frac{1}{4}$-inch cameo and four sterling flowers $20.00

CELERY VASES

OF ALL THE SPECIAL SERVING VESSELS that once graced our grandparents' and our great-grandparents' tables, one seems to have met with general neglect on the part of individuals who are seeking something new to collect. Punch bowls of cut and other glass are eagerly sought. The decorated berry bowl in its marvelous silver or plated frame is adored by multitudes. Castor sets, spoon holders, and sugar shakers are bought up almost as rapidly as they appear in the antiques shops. But there is as yet no cult of the celery vase.

This is at least middling strange, since the decorated glass celery vase once reigned majestically on many a dining table and even now would lend elegance to the finest. Scores were turned out in pattern glass.

Perhaps the reason for its neglect is that we do not think today of stalks of celery ever standing upright and proudly in a vase but visualize them only lying stolidly prone in trays. And certainly celery trays in both cut and pattern glass have numerous devotees. But the celery vase deserves once again to occupy a place of importance, if not on our tables, at least on the shelves of things that we collect.

The celery vases of nearly a century ago were made of much the same kind of glass as were the berry bowls and the pickle castors we so eagerly pursue today. They were turned out in various solid colors of glass, ruby and rose being high among the favorites, and many of them were artistically decorated by enameling, the taste running, as it did with so many glass objects, to flowers. Many were housed in silver and silver-plated stands wrought by artisans with enchanted imaginations. Except for shape, of course, and function, they may be considered as members of the same family to which the berry bowls belong.

John Round & Son, Ltd., of Sheffield, England, which manufactured scores of charming table appurtenances last century, did not neglect the celery vase, and one of the company's rare catalogues illustrates one of molded glass in a rather ornate electroplated stand. American firms in the 1890s offered them along with

Celery vases of 1900, both enameled. Left: rose glass. Right: ruby.

celery trays, pickle castors, and marmalade dishes. The vases are usually 8 to 9 inches high and large enough in diameter to hold many stalks of celery.

Those made of art glass will not be cheap, but when their value is more adequately recognized, the prices certainly will be higher still. Here are a few recently asked prices, some of which seem quite low.

Baccarat, "Amberina Swirl" pattern $35.00

Bohemian glass, ruby, etched design, *ca.* 1875 $40.00

Coralene, diamond-quilted, shaded cherry-white to pink with yellow coralene decoration and off-white casing $450.00

Findlay onyx, cream and silver color $375.00

Francesware $52.50

Marble glass ("Slag," purple) $67.50

Pattern glass, "Actress," *Pinafore* scene $105.00

Pattern glass, "Art" $22.00

Pattern glass, "Ashburton" $55.00

Pattern glass, "Baltimore Pear" $30.00.

Pattern glass, "Barberry" $20.00

Pattern glass, "Bleeding Heart" $20.00

Pattern glass, "Colorado," clear with gold $32.00

Pattern glass, "Cupid and Venus" $33.00

Pattern glass, "Frosted Lion" $50.00

Pattern glass, "Honeycomb," scalloped top, flint $31.50

Pattern glass, "Horn of Plenty," flint $83.00

Pattern glass, "Loop and Dart," round ornaments $32.50

Pattern glass, "Ribbed Palm" $55.00

Pattern glass, "Valencia Waffle," amber $46.50

Pattern glass, "Wild Flower," amber $32.00

CANCELED CHECKS, STOCKS AND BONDS, AND ALLIED MATERIALS

AT THIS MOMENT the whole field of so-called paper Americana is being examined anew. No longer is interest confined strictly to such things as early broadsides, post cards, advertising cards, and quite early examples of the arts of printing, lithography, and calligraphy. This is evidenced by the awakening of an interest within the past few years in—of all things—canceled checks.

Shares of stocks and bonds issued in earlier years, most of them formerly considered not worth the paper they were written on, have also begun moving into collectors' hands.

We'll consider certain other paper Americana, such as theatrical mementos in a subsequent chapter, but let's zero in now on the items mentioned above.

A canceled check is not necessarily simply a canceled check: it may be an autographic document of value. Millions of canceled checks have wended their way through the years to the municipal incinerators—and one result is that flames have consumed hundreds of thousands of dollars worth of valuable signatures. So, astute investment-minded collectors are buying up canceled checks in sizable lots. If, in that lot of checks one purchases for, say $5.00, he finds one with the bold signature of Thomas Wolfe, the literary giant of the thirties, or Erskine Caldwell, the Georgia boy who is still going strong after more books than he himself can recall, the small investment has earned a profit. If one should be encountered with the signature of Albert Einstein or Amelia Earhart or Crawford Long, the profit will be larger. For the great men and women of the past did not only write letters or books or speeches, they also wrote checks—and, if they didn't write them, at least they signed them.

Until the past few years, signatures alone, except extremely rare ones, were considered of only nominal value as autographic materials. But of late their values have risen, and some signatures alone are now bringing as much on the collectors' market as some desirable signed autograph letters brought about a decade ago.

Not long ago a firm specializing in autographs offered a group of bank checks signed by distinguished well-known Americans. The prices ranged from $10 for a partially printed check signed by Gerrit Smith, a Civil War days abolitionist, to $175 for one signed by Ulysses S. Grant!

Those who will profit most by buying canceled bank checks are those who know their history and keep abreast of the news of the day. They will also want to subscribe to some of the autograph catalogues issued periodically by many dealers. Most of these are offered without charge to interested persons, although names of those not making purchases within a reasonable time are likely to be eliminated from the mailing lists.

Lithographed billheads, letterheads, and printed forms representing shares of stocks and bonds are of interest and value for several reasons. One is that many bear lithographed illustrations of stores or buildings that are no longer in existence and thus help to preserve a part of the past. Some represent striking examples of the art of lithography itself.

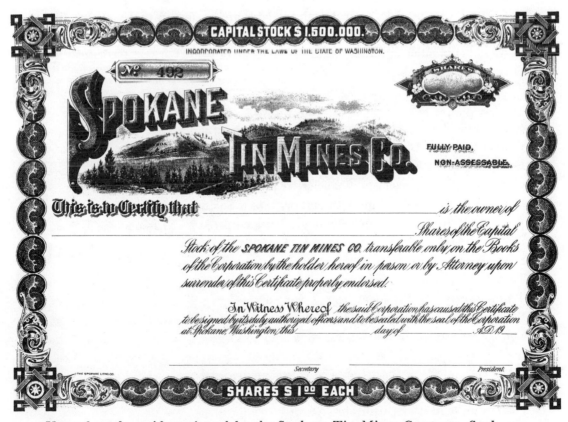

Unused stock certificate issued by the Spokane Tin Mines Company. Such certificates, filled out or blank, are beginning to be collected. Courtesy Jerry Rillahan.

Moreover, many bills of the past list prices that will be of interest in themselves, if for no other reason than for comparison with today's inflated prices, or prices of articles no longer produced but utilized in the past. Researchers find them of interest because they offer clues as to certain types of articles once important in specific geographical localities, perhaps made in those localities.

As for stock and bond certificates, those of greatest interest were issued by types of businesses or ventures that were significant in American history, including types no longer being pursued. These include, for example, stock or bond certificates issued by gold-mining companies, early railroads, horse-drawn-car companies, and firms handling types of mail now handled by the U. S. Postal Service. The best-known of the last category was Wells, Fargo. In a similar category are steamboat bills of lading dating back to the mid-nineteenth century or earlier. Some of these have recently been offered at three for $5.00.

There are numerous other collectible types of paper Americana, but the group listed here contains items that are still easily available, cheap (for the most part), and are likely to rise in value within the next few years. And if they should not, you can always use them for decorating the walls of your den or playroom. Besides, it's always possible, even though the odds are against it, that you may find in that batch of stock certificates or old bonds you acquire one issued by a business still in operation and that could, therefore, be of value.

Here are some values:

BANK CHECKS

Butler, Ellis Parker, American author, 1937 $10.00
Clemens, Samuel G. ("Mark Twain"), American author, 1887 $75.00
Field, Cyrus W., financier, 1878 $15.00
Girard, Stephen, banker and financier, 1830 $50.00
Hawthorne, Nathaniel, American author, 1862 $95.00
Jackson, Andrew, American general and President, 1817 $125.00
Scott, Winfield, United States general, 1851 $15.00
Sheridan, Philip H., United States general, 1879 $25.00
Taft, William H., President, 1919 $50.00
Truman, Harry S., President, 1934 $25.00
Webster, Daniel, statesman, 1835 $25.00
Young, Brigham, Mormon leader, 1872 $75.00

STOCK AND BOND CERTIFICATES

American Merchants Union Express Co., signed by William G. Fargo $50.00
Eastern railroad stock certificate $1.00
Horse-drawn-car company stock certificate $1.50
Miscellaneous stocks and bonds from 1840 through 1920s twenty for $5.00
Pennsylvania Canal Company bonds, $1,000 denomination, 1870 $7.00

Pennsylvania District Corporation 6 per cent loan certificate, engraved in 1853
and including engravings of Benjamin Franklin and William Penn $5.00
Washington & Western Railroad Company bond, $1,000, 1883, with engraving
of locomotive on turntable $9.00

Lithographed letterheads and billheads can be bought in many cases for a
dime to a quarter, although early and scarce examples are now moving higher.

CHARACTER
COLLECTIBLES
FROM BYGONE DAYS

Now that television seems here to stay, everybody misses radio. Nostalgia for that contraption which gave us some of the most fabulous (and some of the most dreadful) entertainment of the century is at a peak, and among its most peculiar manifestations is the collecting of trivia related to numerous programs of those times—particularly the ones featuring characters from the comic strips.

Prices currently being asked for such things as Mickey Mouse watches and the twenty-fifth-century accouterments of Buck Rogers seem incredible. Who, in his right mind, would shell out $200 or so for an Ingersoll wrist watch that Sears, Roebuck sold over its counters during an era that is still remembered by thousands at $1.98, or $100 or more for a windup tin taxicab that was vended at the five-and-ten in 1930? More persons than you might suspect, and those who would like to know why will find the reasons in the book *Collecting Nostalgia,* mentioned earlier.

But simply because there is currently such frantic activity in the realm of these character objects of the thirties and forties, now is the time to seek their predecessors—objects crafted much earlier and made in the likeness of or named after fictional characters created in the nineteenth and early twentieth centuries. The heat on the newer collectibles has taken some of the pressure off the earlier ones, and prevailing prices of the latter may seem quite cheap a few years hence.

We speak now of such remarkable characters as the wondrous Brownies, those tiny sprites whose good-natured pranks amused thousands for many years after 1883 when they were first created by the Canadian-born artist Palmer Cox. Or Buster Brown, introduced in 1902 to readers of the New York *Herald* by the cartoonist R. F. Outcault. Or the Sunbonnet Babies, who sprang from the facile pen of the illustrator Bertha L. Corbett to adorn a series of *Sunbonnet Babies* books written by Eulalie Osgood Grover at the turn of the century and whose antics were thereafter delineated in the ladies' magazines. Or the Kewpies of imaginative Rose O'Neill, who also dabbled in painting, sculpture, prose, and poetry. Through the years literally thousands of articles relating intimately to these and a few other early-day characters have been designed and produced, and some still are being made. All are of interest.

Relatively few of the hundreds of thousands of fictional characters who have been created by writers and artists in the past have survived the decades, but those we have mentioned have. And a multitude of objects have been named after them and are sought widely today. They range from ceramic cups and saucers to silver-plated spoons and from post cards to dolls. They are available from prices of a dollar or two to more than $100.

Early Buster Brown valentines. From the collection of The Historical Society of Buster Brown Comics and Marketing, New York City.

Two years after he had been created, Buster Brown had attained such popularity that the cartoonist Outcault set up a booth at the St. Louis World's Fair and sold the rights to the name to all interested, but only two companies retain the name today—Brown Shoe Company and Buster Brown Textiles, Inc. The president of the latter has established The Historical Society of Buster Brown Comics and Marketing, which also owns a museum of Buster Brown memorabilia at 119 East Thirty-sixth Street, New York City, of which Miss Frances Charman is curator. A few of the numerous Buster Brown collectibles are cigar humidors, leggings, safety match holders, waffle irons, bean-bag game boards, building blocks, numerous booklets, and cigar boxes.

Among the Sunbonnet Babies collectibles the chief focus today is upon a series of ceramic objects produced by the Royal Bayreuth factory in Tettau, Bavaria, the prices of which are substantial. But Sunbonnet Babies ceramics also were made by other factories, and additional collectibles include a variety of advertising gadgets, post cards, Christmas cards, and valentines.

The primary collectible objects in the form of Kewpies are dolls, produced over a period of many years in several substances, including chalk (plaster of paris); but there are also powder jars, ice-cream molds, plates, bowls, figurines, pocket mirrors, tea sets, and so on. The dolls were made both in Europe and the United States of bisque, rubber, celluloid, wood pulp, and plastics. A history of the Kewpies and their creator has been written by Mrs. Rowena Godding Ruggles under the title *The One Rose, Mother of the Immortal Kewpies* (privately printed, Oakland, California). There is also a national Rose O'Neill Club with a membership of more than six hundred. Kewpie dolls are still being produced, but collectors seek those with Rose O'Neill's name on them. Being sought too right now are pages of the various magazines in which the Kewpies appeared.

Palmer Cox's "Brownies at Work," from his Another Brownie Book *of 1890. From the Graham Hunter Collection of Palmer Cox Brownie material.*

Brownies appeared as dolls, decorations on porcelains, figurines of clay and other materials, spoons, paper cutouts, puzzles, and games. A first edition of *The Brownies: Their Book* in mint condition is likely to set the purchaser back about $250. In 1891 the Arnold Print Works of North Adams, Massachusetts, offered a set of twelve Brownie figures printed on a yard of cloth, intended to be cut out, stuffed, and sewed to make stuffed toys. The price was originally $.20 for the yard! The same company offered a large number of other characters on printed cloth, including cats, dogs, monkeys, owls, rabbits, and Little Red Riding Hood. Stuffables made from the cloth or the cloth itself for any of these are currently sleepers.

Whereas these early characters were chiefly good or mildly prankish, the more recent crop includes adventurers, swashbucklers, and daredevils. The more recent extremes are represented by Buck Rogers, whose adventures in the twenty-fifth century have given rise to the creation of miniature marvels of weaponry and spacecraft, and Howdy Doody, the whimsical hero of radio and television. There are no "typical" collectors of these various character objects. They include house-wives, plumbers, department-store executives, milliners, attorneys, and Harvard students. There are so many truly hip collectors of the new character items that it is probably futile to hope to pick up a bargain in them at antiques shows, but there is always the possibility that some of these, as well as some of the other ob-jects with which we have been concerned in this chapter, will be encountered at bargain prices at garage and rummage sales, establishments dealing in second-hand merchandise, and, very occasionally, flea markets. And there is also the very considerable likelihood that stocks of some of these objects are stashed away in storage and that the intrepid trader may be able to purchase the entire stock from an unsuspecting owner who views it largely as scrap. The problem, natu-rally, is to find these stocks—so never pass a shuttered warehouse without at least trying to peep in.

Current values of collectibles discussed in this chapter follow:

BROWNIES (Palmer Cox)

Book, *The Brownies: Their Book,* by Palmer Cox, 1887 $15.00 to $35.00
Calendar, advertising, with Brownie drawings, 5×7 inches $18.00
Candlestick, metal, Irishman $50.00
Cup, ceramic, with Brownie figures $23.00
Drawing, original Brownie drawn on card and signed by Palmer Cox, dated 1898
     $20.00
Figure, Brownie, plaster with movable arms and legs, 5 inches high $20.00
Figure, china, Brownie policeman on match holder $40.00
Fork, child's, with embossed Brownies and dog, plated $10.50
Knife, red celluloid handle with two Brownies and motto $7.00
Paper dolls, Brownies, set of four, premiums $10.00
Pin box, metal, 3¼×1¼ inches, metal, five Brownies on cover $15.00
Plate, ceramic, 8½ inches diameter, sixteen Brownies depicted $32.50
Platter, ceramic, oval, with Brownies $35.00
Salt shaker, Brownies depicted $30.00
Stickpin, enameled Brownies $12.00

Coloring set $3.50

Disintegrator pistol $30.00 to $90.00

Figurines, lead, set of six $24.00

Flash Blast Attack Ship, 4½ inches long $50.00

Helium pistol $50.00

Holster and belt, 1930s $12.00

Knife with three blades $75.00 to $100.00

Magic Transogram pictures in original box $25.00

Mechanical Police Rocket Patrol, Marx toy $45.00

Pin in color $20.00

Pin-back button $13.50

Pocket watch (Ingraham) $225.00 to $275.00

Pop-up book, *Strange Adventures in the Spider Ship,* 1935 $40.00 to $60.00

Solar Scouts, Repeller Ray Ring with "Mystic Emerald" $70.00

Sonic Ray Gun, 9½ inches long, plated, 1940s $20.00 to $25.00

Space Pistol, Wyandotte toy $10.00

Space Ship, wind-up, Marx toy, copyrighted 1927 $25.00

Twenty-fifth Century Daisy Dart Gun $25.00

Twenty-fifth Century Daisy Pistol with holster, 7 inches long $25.00 to $80.00

U-235 Atomic Pistol in original box $75.00

Venus Duo Destroyer Rocket Ship, Tootsietoy $12.50 to $17.50

Water pistol, repeating, mid-1930s $85.00 to $110.00

Zip-Zap pocket pistol, small and large sizes $75.00 to $110.00

BUSTER BROWN

Bank, toy, Buster Brown and Tige, early $47.50

Booklet, *Experiences with Pond's Extract* (advertising), signed Outcault (R. F. Outcault was the creator of the comic strip of this name) $12.50

Button pin, advertising bread $3.50

Dictionary, *Buster Brown Dictionary* $9.00

Fork, figural, silver-plated $8.50

Fork and knife, figural, silver-plated, set $25.00

Mug, depicting Buster and Tige pouring tea $20.00

Plate, ceramic, 5 inches in diameter, transfer print showing Tige balancing kettle on nose $20.00 to $50.00

Pocket knife, with illustration of Buster $17.50

Watch, Ingraham $135.00

Whistle, tin $18.00

HOWDY DOODY

American History Album, promoting Wonder Bread $3.00

Apron $3.00

Howdy Doody dolls and puppets came in many sizes and varied garb. From the collection of Rita Brand.

Crayon set $5.00 to $7.50
Doll, 4 inches tall, movable mouth, plastic $7.50
Hat, peaked at top $4.00

Lunch pail, tin $6.50
Marionette $15.00 to $30.00
Paint set with masks $5.00
Puppet Show, book with punch-out pages to make puppets $25.00
Shoe polish, $3.00
Spoon, long handle $3.00 to $4.00
Sun Ray camera, plastic $10.00
Watch, wrist, automated eyes, Patent Watch Co., $100.00 to $150.00
Wheel Quiz Show Game $4.50
Wind-up toy, tin band $75.00

KEWPIES

Action Kewpie mirror, celluloid $15.00
Bowl, ceramic, signed Rose O'Neill $40.00 to $90.00
Box, tin, depicting swimming Kewpies $22.50
Bisque bride and groom from wedding cake, 2½ inches tall, pair $40.00
Bisque figurine, 6 inches tall, original sticker $50.00
Charm, ivory, 1 inch tall $25.00
Clock, thirty-hour movement, Jasper Ware case by Wedgwood, signed Rose
   O'Neill $200.00
Coaster, ceramic by Royal Rudolstadt, picturing three Kewpies $29.00
Creamer, Jasper Ware, seven pink Kewpies on green ground $98.50 to $115.00
Creamer, ceramic, picturing three Kewpies in German helmets $47.50
Cup (tea) depicting four Action Kewpies, signed R. O'Neill $47.50
Cup and saucer, five Kewpies on cup, two on saucer, signed R. O'Neill Wilson
   $70.00
Door knocker, brass $55.00
Feeding dish, 9 inches diameter, milk glass, signed Rose O'Neill $75.00
Figure, bisque, 4½ inches high, Kewpie holding face in hands $25.00 to
   $60.00
Figure, bisque, 3½ inches high, Kewpie in high top hat $60.00
Flannel, "The Ice Skaters," signed Rose O'Neill $20.00
Handkerchief, 11 inches square, framed, twenty Kewpies $25.00
Hatpin holder, standing Kewpie $39.50
Inkwell, Kewpie holding pen, signed Rose O'Neill $65.00
Knife, sterling, Kewpie on each side of handle $26.00
Magazine page with Kewpies $8.50
Mirror, pocket, 2 inches diameter $12.50
Pitcher, Jasper Ware, white Kewpies on blue ground $95.00
Plate, 7 inches diameter, Royal Rudolstadt, signed R. O'Neill $100.00
Plate, 6 inches diameter with six Action Kewpies $47.50
Post card with Kewpies $5.00 to $17.50

Ring, sterling, marked G. T. Kid $75.00

Spoon, Kewpie figure on handle and enameled picture of Rose O'Neill in bowl, 5 inches long $50.00

Tea set, children's, eleven pieces, Kewpie on each and each signed $350.00

Toothpick holder with enameled Kewpie, glass $45.00

Vase, Jasper Ware, four embossed Kewpies, signed R. O'Neill Wilson $80.00

SUNBONNET BABIES

Bank, cast iron, 7½ inches high $47.50

Bookends, bronze, 1915, pair $40.00

Bowl, cereal, Royal Bayreuth, babies ironing $75.00

Candleholder, saucer-type, Royal Bayreuth, babies hanging wash $147.50

Creamer, 5½ inches high, Royal Bayreuth, babies cleaning $157.50

Dish, covered, oval, Royal Bayreuth, babies mending $127.50

Dish, cereal, 2×6 inches, Royal Bayreuth $112.00

Doorstop, cast iron $17.50

Dresser tray, 11×7 inches, Royal Bayreuth, babies cleaning $122.50

Hair receiver, footed, Royal Bayreuth, babies mending $136.00

Pin tray, 3½×4½ inches, Royal Bayreuth $112.50

Pitcher, 2¾ inches high, Royal Bayreuth, babies mending $70.00

Pitcher, 4½ inches high, Royal Bayreuth, babies ironing $95.00 to $120.00

Plate, 6 inches diameter, Royal Bayreuth, babies washing $65.00 to $85.00

Plate, 7½ inches diameter, Royal Bayreuth $127.50

Planter, 3 inches high, Royal Bayreuth, babies sweeping $137.50

Post card, 1906 $5.00

Salt and pepper shakers, Royal Bayreuth, babies cleaning and fishing, unsigned, pair $77.50

Sugar bowl, covered, 3 inches high, Royal Bayreuth $150.00

Tea tile, Royal Bayreuth, babies ironing $85.00

Vase, 3 inches high, gold top, Royal Bayreuth $125.00

Waste bowl, Royal Bayreuth $150.00

CIGARETTE PAPER CASES, HOLDERS, AND SAFETY MATCH BOXES

SINCE NICOTINE has been getting such a bad press in recent years, and the fragrant weed seems headed the way of the pomander and the whalebone busk, it is high time we examined some adjuncts of smoking that have been out of sight and largely out of mind for a generation. Such, for example, as the cigarette paper case.

These receptacles were once utilized to hold the filmy papers in which tobacco was rolled to make a cigarette. These cases are now rarities since few of us any longer roll our own, and this art today is confined largely to the cowboys who

Sterling-silver cigarette paper case by Unger Brothers, ca. 1900.

cavort on our television screens. Actually, the cowboys never used the cases; they kept their papers with their tobacco sacks. But the cases were used by city folk, and the silver manufacturers catered to their needs by devising some elegant ones of sterling silver. These were in fairly widespread use prior to World War I, though they were being made well before that.

Cigarette papers came in a standard size early in the century, "longs," "extra-longs," and "thins" not having been invented yet by either the tobacco processors or the advertising agencies; and the cases were also designed of a fairly standard size to accommodate them. Most were fitted with a snap lock so they could be easily opened. Some magnificent chased, embossed, and engraved sterling cases were available for smokers who could afford them at the beginning of this century, and certainly some could be classed, without stretching a point, as miniature works of art. Lesser ones were electroplated and could be afforded by the masses, or at least those of the masses who preferred to and were able to roll their own cigarettes. Not everyone was, because cigarette rolling required practice and some skill. The true experts could roll a cigarette with the fingers of a single hand, but others needed the assistance of a small and simple mechanism in order to roll the flimsy paper around a short length of tobacco. Almost anyone, however, could lick the edge of the paper and seal it around to make a little tube.

Some cigarette papers (corn husks were used at one time for this purpose) came in booklet form, and it was a simple matter to insert these into the cigarette paper cases. For a good many years, the tobacco manufacturers issued the paper booklets with their small bags of tobacco, and one obtained with each sack of tobacco enough papers to make four more cigarettes than are now contained in the standard pack.

By World War II, cigarette paper cases were rapidly disappearing because of the convenience of packaged cigarettes, although around 1943, when cigarettes were getting hard to come by, inexpensive roll-your-own machines came on the market. The paper cases, however, were not revived. The abundantly decorated silver paper cases are now a part of the American past, and they deserve a far better fate than the scrap heap. Several astute antiques dealers around the country are now seeking them out, and the individual collector can take a tip from them: buy them now before the prices zoom.

The long cigarette holder, an offspring of the cigar holder, undoubtedly helped inspire the long cigarette. Now that there's such a hullabaloo about nicotine and tar, cigarette holders are making a comeback. They were never really abandoned but their use diminished sharply when filter-tipped cigarettes appeared. Prior to that, no one gave much of a thought to nicotine and tar but a good many people were irritated by the little wisps of tobacco that invariably were extruded from the smoking tip of the cigarette onto the lips and into the mouth. Cigarette holders prevented that, and women were in the majority among their users.

Both cigarette and cigar holders have been made of such substances, in addition to amber, as synthetic amber, ivory, meerschaum, and Bakelite. The finer holders boasted sterling-silver trimmings or 14-karat gold bands. There were collapsible cigarette holders made in sections that folded into one another much in the manner of collapsible cups and that had their own small sterling-silver or gold-filled carrying cases. Some choice ones of this type were selling in 1915 at $4.00 to $5.00. And holders that ejected the smoked cigarettes were around early in the century, one well-known brand whose popularity continued over a number of years having been Ejekto.

Some of the early cigar holders are pippins, and the most delightful of all are those decorated with molded figures. Most of these had holder sections of meerschaum and amber mouthpieces. The favorite figures were those of horses and dogs. These figural meerschaum and amber holders were customarily sold in velvet-lined cases that protected them when not in use. Their designs parallel those of the charming figural meerschaum pipes, and large numbers were made in Germany, Austria, and France.

There were also pipe-shaped cigarette holders, some 10 inches long and featuring cloudy or transparent colors. During the 1920s they could be bought for less than half a dollar.

A collection of great diversity could be assembled of cigarette and cigar holders dating from the latter part of the nineteenth century.

We discussed advertising match safes in an earlier chapter, and match safes in general are widely sought, but little attention has been paid thus far to the little boxes designed to hold safety matches. Yet there is no reason why these are not fully as collectible as the safes, and, although they were not made in as great a variety of designs as the latter, their diversity is sufficient to enable a satisfying collection to be made.

Among the larger makers of the sterling-silver match boxes in the second decade of this century was the Elgin American Manufacturing Company, a firm that also produced lighters, cigarette cases, and vanity cases. The majority of match boxes were squarish in shape with a cut-out portion of metal on one side so that the matches could be struck against the abrasive side of the cardboard boxes. The cases of the boxes were decorated by various methods, including embossing. Some fancy ones were embossed with floral and other designs. An absolutely captivating type was the figural holder, produced in sterling silver early in the century by Unger Brothers. One of their match-box holders was made in the shape of an owl's head and another, the head of a hound dog. Either of these could well be the high point of a collection.

Many match-box holders were made as part of ashtrays, usually attached to one side. In addition to sterling, the holders were made of plate, brass and copper.

It should also be mentioned in passing that paper and cardboard cigarette packages are also beginning to be collected. One reason is that their designs have changed sharply through the years. In addition, numerous brands once made are no longer being manufactured. (In the case of Lucky Strikes, the material used in making the early green packs was needed for war use in the forties and was diverted from commercial use.) Full packages of cigarettes are worth more than empty ones, but some empty packs are bringing as much as $5.00! And early lighters are a challenge to collect, as they are scarce.

Sterling-silver figural match-box holders by Unger Brothers.

The articles discussed in this chapter still constitute sleepers, and choice examples may still be obtained at bargain prices if one is willing to search for them. The match-box holders are rarely advertised but should be available now in a price range of $2.00 for simple ones to as much as $15 or $20 for fine ones of sterling. Many cigarette paper cases are obtainable for $3.00 or $4.00 to $20 or so, depending upon the material of which they are made and their quality.

Here are some typical prices being asked for holders:

Art Deco design, case illustrated with man in tuxedo and top hat $12.00
German amber cigar holder in case 2¼ inches long $12.00

Ivory cigar holder with carved baboon and baby, in case $35.00
Meerschaum and amber cigar holder in plush case $9.00 to 20.00
Silver-plated holder by Victor Silver Co., claw feet $9.00
Silver-plated holder, plain $7.00
Silver-plated holder with 14-karat gold band $10.00

COLD CREAM, SALVE, AND TALCUM POWDER JARS AND PICTORIAL HAND MIRRORS

MANY OF THOSE small and often captivating vessels that once housed creams, salves, powder, unguents, and the like have become fair game for the collector, and a judiciously chosen assemblage of them could prove profitable if held for a relatively short time, say two or three years.

Small glass jars to hold cold cream and skin salves, including Vaseline, were

Glass salve boxes, ca. 1900. One at top left has gold-plated top.

in widespread use last century, and they continued to decorate milady's dressing table through the early 1900s. The finest were made of cut glass and had sterling tops, richly engraved. Some tops were produced with stones, such as amethysts, inlaid in them. These are scarce today but well worth seeking.

Many of the jars were round, but a large number were made in square and octagonal shapes. In addition to cut glass, some were produced in plain crystal and silver. Simpson, Hall, Miller & Company, Wallingford, Connecticut, designed and marketed a series of unusual Vaseline jars of plated silver lavishly embossed with floral designs, some footed and others accompanied by silver-plated stands. These stood 4 to 5 inches high and wholesaled early in this century at prices of $2.50 to $3.25.

M. S. Benedict Manufacturing Company marketed a group of salve and pomade jars of pressed glass made in imitation of cut glass with silver-plated tops.

It is interesting to note that a large percentage of the salve, pomade, and Vaseline jars were made in patterns that duplicated those created for hair receivers and puff boxes of the same period. Tops, too, often utilized the same patterns.

Pictorial-back hand mirror with gold-plated mountings by M. S. Benedict Manufacturing Company, early twentieth century. Mirror is 5 inches in diameter.

Pictorial-back sterling hand mirror by Unger Brothers, showing Art Nouveau influence.

Talcum powder jars were made of the same types of glass but were much taller as were tooth powder jars, or bottles. These also had sterling tops. In 1918 the St. Louis Clock & Silverware Company offered a diversity of cut-glass tooth powder, talcum, Vaseline, and salve jars with sterling tops with suggested retail prices of $.70 to $3.00 each!

Thousands of delightful small hand mirrors with pictorial backs in both hand-painted porcelain and silver that would grace any boudoir today were manufactured about the turn of this century. Why these have thus far been neglected is a mystery. If the mirror surfaces are in poor condition, they can be resilvered, and one can make a beautiful display of them in addition to using them for their original purpose. Various types of scenes, including seascapes and landscapes, depictions of children and nymphs were used on these mirror backs. During the early years of the century mirrors with Art Nouveau decoration appeared, with Unger Brothers among the larger manufacturers. Some of these hand mirrors were fantastic. Of equal interest are the decorated pocket mirrors of the same period, many of which were also decorated in the Art Nouveau style. Stylized flowers, cherubs, sinuous females, and Indians predominate as decorative motifs.

Very few of the boudoir accouterments mentioned here are being collected to any extent at the present with the result that many of them undoubtedly still remain in homes that have been stripped by antiques dealers and collectors of most of their other antiques. And private homes are the best place to search for them. You can probably pick them up now for a trifling sum as compared with their value—and what they'll be selling for in a very few years.

Since so few of these items have been advertised for sale, we are not including a list of prices here. However, the writer has encountered some of them in a few antiques shops. The salve, pomade, and Vaseline jars in cut glass with original sterling tops will sell for $7.50 to $17.50, but those of crystal have been encountered at prices of $3.50 to $7.50. Crystal or pressed-glass tooth powder jars may be found for as little as $3.00 to $5.00. A few mirrors have been priced at $10 to $25 in good condition; those with mirror surfaces in poor condition can occasionally be located at a price of under $10.

COLLAPSIBLE CUPS

THOSE WHO CAN FIGURE OUT why fads develop stand to make a fortune. Sometimes fads take wings for no apparent reason, and frequently the fad involves the insignificant. Like collapsible cups.

Advertisements seeking these sectioned drink holders are already trickling into the collector periodicals. More have appeared within the past year than had appeared for the preceding ten years. Before long collapsible cups may be taking on values of which their original producers never dreamed.

These cups, originally called collapsion cups, date back to the bicycle riding days of last century (and bicycle riding, it is worth noting in passing, has also come back into popularity). And they were in use up to fairly recent times. Moreover, they are not all nearly so prosaic as one might suspect, competition among manufacturers apparently having stimulated some imaginative designing and packaging.

Most collapsible (or collapsion, take your pick) cups were made of metal segments that telescoped into one another when the cup was not being used, thereby making it convenient to tote about. Cyclists who wouldn't have dreamed of packing a glass tumbler on their boneshakers would take along a collapsible cup with the greatest of ease. Collapsible cups were also a boon to picnickers whose baskets were cramped for space, and they came in awfully handy during Prohibition days for folk who toted their flasks in their hip pockets but preferred to drink from something other than the bottle.

A variety of collapsible cups were manufactured almost immediately after the enactment of our Prohibition laws. There were swank ones of plated silver, some embossed and satin-engraved, some with handles, some without, and the majority accompanied by a small leather carrying case that could fit neatly into the pocket of a man's coat or jacket or into a lady's purse. Some handles, such as reversible ones, were protected by patent.

Silver-plated collapsible cups with cases were retailing soon after the outbreak

Collapsible cups, pre-World War I. From top: cup with patented reversible handle; nested drinking cups in seal-grain leather case; reversible-handle cup shown packed in leather case.

of World War I at prices of from $3.00 up. A plain one in a grained walrus-leather case could be had for around $3.50, or a polished handled one for $5.50. One of sterling silver with a cover housed in a leather case could cost $13 to $15, however. Some merchandise catalogues of that era illustrate collapsible cups on the same pages with flasks.

For those who wanted the cups but didn't have much to spend, they were available in polished nickel for a dollar up. In fact, one of nickel in a grained seal-leather case cost just that. You couldn't buy the case alone for a dollar today.

Some of the cases were jazzed up a bit too, featuring silver mountings, and these were even available for the nickel cases, though the price was a couple of dollars or more.

For couples who wanted to spend a quiet evening alone with a bottle of cheer, collapsible cups were offered in pairs, one just small enough to fit inside the other and the two nesting in a leather case. Aluminum cups cost about the same as those of nickel. In the twenties nested drinking cups with detachable handles were made of brass plated with nickel and came in sets of two, four, or six. A cover on the top cup held the nest together, and these were ideal for picnics and camping trips.

The average collapsible cup measured about 2 inches high when it had been opened and the sections snapped together and about 2½ inches in diameter at the top.

We won't attempt to explain what now appears to be the beginning of a fad for collapsible cups of earlier days but merely report it to readers, some of whom may wish to speculate by buying up a few and then waiting to see if there is a full-blown craze before long.

Virtually all the ads thus far have been for collapsible cups wanted and not for sale, so no prices have been established. One should be able to pick them up now for a very few dollars if they are in good condition and without rust. A fair range should be $3.00 to about $10.00.

DOOR KNOCKERS, DINNER GONGS, AND BELLS

As a result of ex-President Nixon's historic visit to China, the artifacts of that country are taking off price-wise on one of history's greatest sprints.

Chinese porcelains, pottery, bronzes, sculptures, and what the auction houses love to term *objets de vertu* are coveted by those who can afford them and those who can't, and the former are out to amass these treasures in the largest possible quantities and at the earliest possible time. Entire auctions are now being devoted to oriental antiquities supplemented by more recent objects of something less than *vertu,* with emphasis on things Chinese, and friend is bidding against friend for them, right down to the last million dollars.

It becomes obvious, then, that it will prove futile for the impoverished collector to seek for bargains among these treasures. But if he is determined to have something with the stamp of China on it, then let him consider a class of objects that few seem to have considered as yet and which he can come by for a sum enormously less than that required to purchase a Shang Dynasty ritual bronze or a Yang-Shoa decorated pottery funerary jar of the neolithic period. We speak of the brass gongs once utilized to summon folk to dinner.

Tea bells, cast-iron brass and dinner bells, and farm bells that summoned hands from the field to the kitchen are all collectible and collected, and yet none of these is quite as intriguing as the dinner gong, particularly the figural variety.

Huge gongs were used in the Orient many decades ago for a great variety of purposes, but smaller gongs for the table, of more recent vintage, can be fully as fascinating—and annoying—and today they are rarely seen. It is interesting to note that such small gongs were popular in England in the nineteenth century as trophies or as presentation gifts in recognition of some accomplishment or service.

The simplest of these gongs consists of a round brass plate hung between uprights attached to a base. They are accompanied (or should be) by strikers, sometimes of wood, sometimes of metal, and, advisedly, covered with cloth. Small gongs of this type were in use in a good many homes in this country early in the century, and in 1915 they were selling for $5.00 and up.

Brass figural gongs with brass or wooden hammers were made in China and exported to the United States in 1930; other types, however, had been exported much earlier, and these included some quite large ones—far too large for use atop a dining table, but admirably suited to other purposes, such as calling lodge meetings to order and otherwise shattering the peace and quiet of a lovely evening.

Chinese dinner gongs of the type imported by United States businesses years ago.

The brass gongs, and especially the figural ones, hold interest for bell collectors and for collectors of brass, but they will also appeal to a much wider audience once their winsomeness is noted. Many of the gongs are decorated with dragons, some of which are enameled, and many stands were made in striking figural forms, such as pairs of elephants or warriors, holding the metal gong between them.

Among the collectible dinner gongs of the twenties are bell-shaped ones supported by metal rings or cast figures of exotic birds. The smaller gongs make excellent conversation pieces and certainly can be put to good use in summoning the family to dinner.

Of course not all of these gongs were made in China; they were made all over the East, including Japan, Thailand, Cambodia, and India, and the earliest ones do date back centuries, but these age-old ones will be beyond the grasp of most readers. The more recent ones will not, and whether they were actually crafted in China or not makes no particular difference if you wish to collect them for their own sake and not for the sake of riding the coattail of current fashion. Usually you will find the brass gongs cheaper than those of bronze. Gongs also

Brass figural door knockers from a salesman's sample catalogue of the last century.

were made of stone long ago, and rare and precious ones of jade, but these, too, are out of place in a discussion of types that can be put to current usage.

I have collected several gongs, ranging from those of very small size that can stand with ease on a table top to those measuring about 18 inches in diameter on stands 2½ feet tall, and I put them to therapeutic use. When I arise in the morning in ill humor and filled with frustrations and worries, all I need do to restore my customary buoyancy and set the world aright is to pick up one of their strikers and shatter the quiet of the daybreak hour and the peace of the neighborhood.

It should be noted in passing that the door knocker, which has now largely given way to the raucous electric buzzer, is also due for a revival. The small and impersonal electrically controlled button that currently languishes sentinel-like beside our entrance doors performs the chore assigned it but is utterly lacking in elegance or character and cannot hold a candle to the pleasant and sometimes bewitching door knocker of yore. Early vintage door knockers are being collected, and among the choice ones are those of iron or brass in shapes such as those of lions, elephants, dogs, historical personalities, effigies, monsters, and heraldic emblems.

I'm reminded of these because I have just come into possession of several pages of designs for door knockers, apparently dated about seventy-five or eighty years ago and obviously from a salesman's or a designer's book. Represented are knockers featuring busts of such personalities as Shakespeare, Sir Walter Raleigh, Lord Byron, kings, religious leaders, climbing bears, a skull and crossbones, a Cheshire cat, knights in armor, musicians, public buildings, and even a Peeping Tom. Any of these would be a delight affixed to the entrance door of a modern home.

Here are a few current prices of gongs with some door knockers thrown in for good measure:

GONGS

Brass gong 5 inches in diameter, flanked by pair of brass axes, 11 inches high on wooden stand $27.50

Brass gong, 6 inches in diameter, engraved with Chinese characters, on base of dark wood, 12 inches tall $35.00

Brass gong 6 inches in diameter, supported by two carved wooden elephants 16 inches tall, on wooden base 20 inches long $75.00

Brass gong 16 inches in diameter, supported by wooden posts 24 inches tall, with cloth-wrapped wooden striker $125.00

Brass gong 18 inches in diameter, supported by wooden uprights 24 inches tall, with wooden striker $175.00

DOOR KNOCKERS

Brass hand holding ball, lacy cuff-ring on finger $35.00

Brass lion's head with ring, 6×9 inches, unpolished $20.00 to 50.00
Brass rabbit $10.00
Brass bust of Shakespeare $20.00
Cast-iron basket of flowers $7.50 to 12.50
Cast-iron figure of "Betty Boop" (1930s) $15.00
Cast-iron parrot $15.00
Cast-iron teardrop shape, engraved $10.00

EPERGNES,
FLOWER STANDS,
FIGURAL NUT BOWLS
AND NUTCRACKERS,
AND JELLY DISHES

THERE IS AN OLD SAYING to the effect that a dinner lubricates business, and there is a new saying to the effect that an interestingly appointed table lubricates a bad dinner.

Aside from formal affairs, there is rarely a focal point of interest on today's dining tables—except for the food itself; and it is high time for the revival of the epergne, the flower stand, the figural bowl, and those utterly delightful containers once made for jelly, jam, and marmalade.

The silver epergne in America dates back to colonial days and was a reflection of the owner's social standing or wealth. The glass epergne came later and was far less costly. Its popularity lasted from the middle of the last century to about 1900 when it, in turn, gave way to colorful fruit or berry bowls, small versions of which are called brides' baskets.

At the moment, fruit and berry bowls in ornate frames are being earnestly collected, and prices have risen to the point where a first-rate berry bowl and frame will set one back $75 to $250. Meanwhile, the glass epergne languishes. It does so without rhyme or reason, because many epergnes are admirable examples of the glassmaker's art. At today's low prices for large numbers of them, they should be excellent investments, looking toward their revival for gracing once again the dining table, or, for that matter, just about any room in one's home.

Epergnes of glass were produced at some of this country's most noted glasshouses, including the Boston and Sandwich factory. They were made through the years in many forms, the most commonly seen featuring one or more "lilies" in vaselike form rising from a bowl with a base. Some epergnes had two bowls, or even more, and featured glass dishes instead of the lily vases. They were made of cut and decorated glass, including satin glass, Burmese, and other types of art and shaded glass.

The table flower stands were similar, and some extremely interesting ones were made late in the last century by John Round of Sheffield, whom we have mentioned earlier. These had bowls and vases supported by electroplated metal bases in various figural shapes. Those boasting both bowls and vases were used for fruit as well as flowers.

Some simple, single-lily epergnes have gone begging of late for as little as $25 or $35, and, although many more elaborate ones are priced higher, the collector has an opportunity now to acquire them at a figure below their actual worth.

And when it comes to imparting verve to the dining table, the large figural nut bowl can play an important role. Most of these were made of ceramics or metal; those of major interest to collectors will probably be the ones decorated with a molded figure of a squirrel. Nut bowls were crafted by numerous ceramic and silver manufacturers between 1880 and 1920. Those bowls in majolica are highly attractive because of their colors. Some bowls were made in glass, but they are outnumbered by those of metal. An 1898 catalogue of S. F. Myers Company, wholesale jewelers of New York City, illustrates a nut bowl of plated silver, gold-

lined, that would be a collector's prize. It is in the form of half a nutshell, the top rim jagged, on an oval footed base with a handle. Atop the rim stands a bushy-tailed squirrel cracking a nut in its mouth. This bowl was manufactured by the Meriden Britannia Company.

A silver-plated nut dish in the shape of a footed leaf on the stem of which sits a squirrel with a nut is pictured in the 1910 catalogue of Wallenstein, Mayer & Company, now Harry Greenwold, Wallenstein, Mayer, of Cincinnati. It, too, was gold-lined. Another silver-plated bowl offered in 1900 in a catalogue bearing the imprint of D. V. Hembree, of Roanoke, Georgia, consisted of a deep engraved basin with two squirrels seated on the rim.

Nonfigural nut bowls in silver and plated silver were also produced early in this century in a great many sizes and shapes, some lavishly embossed, produced by, among others, Simpson, Hall, Miller & Company of Wallingford, Connecticut.

Following World War I, the production of nut bowls continued, but they were chiefly chaste and prim, and many were made of wood.

The nutcracker, of course, is a vital adjunct of the nut bowl, and virtually no one collects these now; but there are figural and novelty nutcrackers that practi-

Figural nut bowls of gold-lined plated silver, 1890s.

cally yearn to be collected. About 1918 the stores were offering a combination nutcracker and bowl of cast metal. The cracker was the screw type, and a large molded squirrel served as the handle. Early types of nutcrackers were much bulkier than the more recent ones. A table nutcracker of 1900 had small metal points protruding from the flat surfaces on which the nuts were cracked when the handles were squeezed. Figural nutcrackers were made in the shapes of dogs, squirrels, roosters, cats, and even human busts.

Finally, a revival of interest is overdue in the novelty jam, jelly, and marmalade jars and their stands of earlier years. Late nineteenth-century marmalade dishes

of cut glass in silver-plated frames could grace the most elegant table. Some sterling frames were made to house marmalade jars of glass and were offered complete with spoon. Magnificent jelly bowls of cut glass were made during the "Brilliant period," but, as is the case with so much of the cut glass of these years, the prices are relatively high.

Scores of different types of jam jars in glass were made during the first two decades of this century. Some were accompanied by saucers or underplates. There were jars of "rock-crystal," jars decorated with sterling-silver overlay, jars with silver-plated tops, crystal jelly dishes that resembled small versions of the covered butter dish, combination glass-lined jelly dishes and silver-plated biscuit trays, glass marmalade jars in Sheffield openwork-handled frames that resembled steins, and glass jars in openwork metal frames with bails. There were engraved jelly-glass liners in pierced frames with engraved covers. The Webster Company

Figural nutcrackers. Left: Buddhist monk, carved possibly in France or the former French Indochina area; nuts are cracked in a recess back of the head. Right: Italian carved walnut. Courtesy Sam A. Cousley and The Cousley Collections and SPINNING WHEEL.

marketed a variety of decorated glass marmalade jars with hand-engraved and enameled silver-plated tops, some housed in individual plush-lined cases, together with a spoon.

Around the turn of the century Unger Brothers offered a group of beautifully decorated china jam pots with sterling-silver tops and spoons in elaborate plush-lined cases, any of which would be a collector's dream.

Check the shelves and tables of antiques shops for jam and jelly jars in tarnished holders: if sterling, these can be restored to gleaming beauty by silver polish. So can plated ones whose silver coat has not worn through. You are not likely to find many, but you may find some at quite low prices since there are still a few antiques dealers who don't check all the metal objects they acquire carefully enough to determine whether they are made of sterling or undamaged plate.

Here are a few recent prices:

EPERGNES (GLASS)

Blue opalescent, hobnail pattern with three lilies $36.50
Clear to opalescent, four lilies $72.00
Cranberry, single lily 10¾ inches tall, filigree around stem $75.00
Cranberry, three 6-inch-tall lilies on silver-plated stand $110.00
Sandwich glass type, single lily 5½ inches tall, white-frosted $17.50
Vaseline opalescent, single lily 9 inches tall in silver-plated holder $35.00

NUT BOWLS AND DISHES

Plated silver, 1½ inches tall, 5 inches in diameter, two handles marked Tufts
   $15.00
Plated silver, three-sectioned with squirrel finial $30.00
Sterling silver, 6⅜ inches diameter, decorated with grapes and leaves $35.00

NUTCRACKERS

Brass Cheshire cat $18.00
Brass dog $35.00
Brass rooster's head $12.00
Cast-iron dog $8.50 to 25.00
Cast-iron "Home Nut Cracker," patented 1915 $6.50
Cast-iron pecan cracker, patented 1913 $6.50
Cast-iron "Perfection," patented 1914 $6.50
Cast-iron squirrel $5.00 to 15.00
Metal, "Alex," patented 1913 $4.00
Wooden, hand-carved head of President Rutherford B. Hayes, 8½ inches long
   $35.00

FIRE GRENADES

THE ACTIVITIES OF THE BOTTLE COLLECTOR apparently go on around the clock. Bottle buffs will spend their weekends, holidays, and vacations pursuing their hobby from city dumps to country outhouses.

One type of collectible bottle that has not yet been so widely popularized as to make its price prohibitive is the glass fire extinguisher, some versions of which were called "fire grenades" because of their method of use and resemblance in shape to military grenades. These heavy glass grenades and similar bottles were filled with carbon tetrachloride, a colorless liquid used to help extinguish fires. Most of them came with wall brackets so they could be hung in handy places around the home or office. If a small fire originated, the bottle was thrown with force into the flames, where it broke and its contents were released to smother the blaze.

Although these bottle extinguishers are said to have been around earlier, their heyday was in the 1880s and 1890s. Among the earliest and most widely known brands was Harden's Fire Grenade. Many of these bottles were variously embossed "Harden's Hand Grenade Fire Extinguisher," "Harden's Hand Fire Extinguisher, Grenade," and so on, often accompanied by a patent date and some with a large star and the word "Star." They have been found in amber, green, and several shades of blue glass, a number of them patterned with ribbing or quilted diamonds.

There were several other brands of this same basic type of fire extinguisher, including Hayward, a New York firm; Harkness, made by the General Fire Extinguisher Company, New York; Diamond, Korbeline, Rockford Kalamazoo, and Magic Film, to mention only some. I have one that is a salesman's sample with a printed floating strip inside lettered "Red Comet Demonstration Grenade —Not to Be Sold." It was purchased at auction a couple of years ago for $4.00. This bottle is completely sealed with a pontil on the base, but others had cork closures firmly sealed.

Probably the majority of those produced have been lost to today's collectors by virtue of having been tossed into fires, but some are still available and make valuable additions to a bottle collection. Some of the rarer types will fetch prices of $40 up, but many have been seen recently at prices of $7.50 to $25. The best place to locate these is probably in the "For sale" columns of the collector periodicals and at bottle shows.

Some recently advertised prices follow:

Auto Fyrstop with wall bracket $11.00
Clear glass, grenade-shaped, unmarked, with wall bracket $7.50
Cobalt blue glass, unidentified $12.50
Harden's Hand Grenade, sapphire blue or turquoise $25.00 to 75.00
Harden's three-section grenade, amber, clear, and cobalt blue $60.00
Kalamazoo Automatic & Hand Fire Extinguisher, cobalt blue $45.00
Red Comet with wall bracket $8.50 to 15.00
Shur-Stop, red glass with tin holder $10.00 to 12.50

FISHING ADJUNCTS

FISHING AS A HOBBY antedates Izaak Walton, but with the publication in 1653 of *The Compleat Angler; or The Contemplative Man's Recreation*, Walton did more than any man before his time or since to popularize the sport. And if you possess a copy of the first edition of that book, you needn't look elsewhere for an investment: you already have a small fortune in your hands. But if you don't and

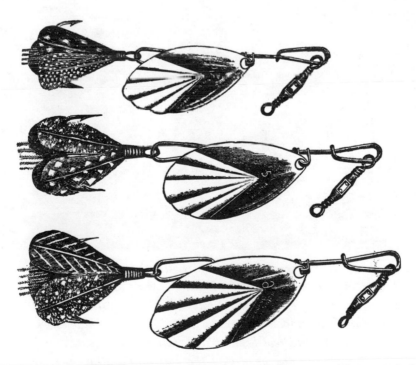

Nickel-plated bait from the Belknap Hardware Company, early twentieth century.

Rare reels, bait casters (second row from bottom), and other equipment from the collection of Richard Miller of Hudson, Mass. A rare early metal lure, patented in 1852 by J. T. Buel of Whitehall, N.Y., is shown second from left on the second row from top. The famous B. F. Meek #4 trout reel is seen at left in the center row. An odd reel (center row, extreme left) patented by A. Coates on March 20, 1888, is unusual in that the entire unit attaches to a rod with a button catch. Photo courtesy Richard Miller.

116

if fishing is your recreation, you have an opportunity to combine it with collecting to advantage.

Fishing adjuncts, particularly lures, are high on the list of imminent antiques. And, for a starter, you might try looking in the tackle boxes of some of your more elderly fishermen companions.

The bamboo-pole-and-bait-worm fisherman is still with us, but there are not nearly so many of these around as there were a century ago. There have been hundreds of innovations in artificial bait throughout this century, and there are more to come. These have outmoded their predecessors, and there are undoubtedly many lures whose brand names are unfamiliar to today's younger fishermen. These are collectible right now and many can be picked up for a pittance. By tomorrow their value is likely to have risen considerably.

Heddon is an old name in fish lures, and the Heddon "Dowagiac" minnows, which were made in colors from sienna-yellow to red, were in widespread use at the turn of the century. So were other brands long since replaced by newer names. Literally carloads of minnows, spinners, and trolling spoons by which good fishermen swore in past years have been abandoned in favor of the constant stream of newcomers. For while some of the old-timers swear by the tackle they have used for years, others rush to try each innovation as soon as it hits the market.

A collection of minnows in color could provide the basis for an admirable collection. So could an assortment of casting reels or fishing-tackle catalogues. There has been a trickle of advertisements for the latter in the collector periodicals within the past year, and these old trade catalogues do not come cheap. More available, however, are early hardware catalogues with sections devoted to fishing tackle.

So, if the subject interests you, why not look out for the "Phantom Minnow," the Pfleuger "Pal-o-Mine," or some of the numerous early Heddon lures? A group of obsolete wooden fishing lures was recently offered at $1.00 each and miscellaneous old spinners at the same price. The lures can make a conversation-sparking display along a wall of your den, and that's more than you can say with "the one that got away."

One ardent collector of fishing tackle is Richard Miller, of Hudson, Massachusetts. He specializes in the old reels and has acquired more than 450 of them during the past five years. There are no duplicates in his collection, which will give an idea of the numerous types made.

In addition, Mr. Miller possesses 150 different early lures, several outstanding rods, and about fifty scarce fishing-gear catalogues.

PENS, PENCILS, AND TYPEWRITERS

THANKS TO THE ADVENT of electronic devices that continue to make the machine masters of men, another age-old art may be on its way out: letter writing. The manual typewriter has seen its happiest days and electric ones may eventually become victim to devices that automatically transcribe dictation. Sadder still, those decorative and once almost essential articles known as "shopping lists" have already disappeared into the mists of time.

In short, those implements that have enabled us to indulge in what has been termed the language of the hand are falling before the onslaught of the machine, thereby creating an entirely new category of antiques.

During the past century and a half a revolution has occurred in pens. The goose quill yielded to the shaft with a metal point, the dip pen to the barrel-filled fountain pen, the fountain pen to the ball point. The cartridge-using pen has virtually eliminated the need for the ink bottle, now the apple of the eye of many a collector. Even early fountain pens, by no means yet antique, have become collectible as have those fascinating gold and silver pencils of a few decades ago, and the "shopping lists" or memo tablets once attached by pin to milady's blouse or worn on her chatelaine, that safe-keeper of dainty and useful small articles.

Right now those early fountain pens, especially those that made their appearance about the turn of the century, are being retrieved from the dump heaps and examined anew with curiosity. And mechanical pencils of the midget variety are being sought in the recesses of dresser drawers and attic-stored trunks.

We will not belabor the matter of fountain pens here except to suggest that readers watch for those in telescopic cases, those with silver and rolled-gold barrels, and novel types with nineteenth-century patent dates.

Of as much or more interest, however, are the small gold and silver pencils in scores of shapes, sizes, and designs that seem to have been made by the carload early in the twentieth century and a few years before. They included mechanical

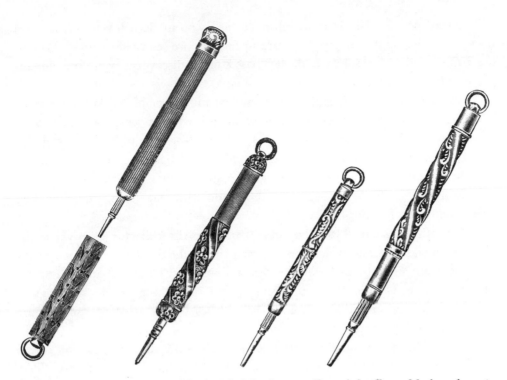

Early twentieth century gold-plated Magic pencils originally sold for $33 to $36 a dozen wholesale. Those of sterling were $15 to $18 a dozen.

ones whose points screwed into the barrels and with small rings at one end so they could be attached to chatelaines or fastened to the blouse with a pin. Two-part silver pencils that could be pulled apart and the sections reversed for writing appeared early in the century as did larger gold, sterling, and nickel-silver clutch pencils with pocket clips and retractable points, combination pencils and Waldemar chains, and combination pencils and four-foot-long silk ribbons. A collector's item is a combination retractable-point pencil-knife, the blade of the knife housed in the upper portion of the combination's barrel.

Since these things appear trifles, the reader may wonder at this point whether there will ever be serious collectors of them. Wonder no more. Jack Harcrow, a retired railroad man of Cartersville, Georgia, has pioneered the pen and pencil field and has amassed a fantastic collection of them from over the world. He started out by seeking fountain pens with advertising lettered on them but ended up an eclectic collector, who also latched onto lap desks, paperweights, and letter openers. Included in his collection of pencils are two that represented experiments by a pencil manufacturing company, which informed him that it had invested $50,000 in the production of just ten pencils.

There is also an American Pencil Collectors' Society with headquarters in Sterling, Kansas.

The lead pencil, Mr. Harcrow informed me, is no modern invention; it dates back to the sixteenth century. It is rare to find a pure lead pencil now, those in use being made of graphite and clay based on a discovery by a Frenchman, Jacques Conte, in 1795.

A companion collectible is the silver-handled ink eraser of the late nineteenth and early twentieth centuries. These erasers consisted of a scraping blade and a decorated handle, some of which were of mother-of-pearl trimmed with sterling. It may be interesting to note that these were "stock" handles, used interchangeably for ink erasers, corn knives, letter seals, manicure files, and even hair curlers and toothbrushes. Some erasers were also made with stag horn, simulated stag horn, and ebony handles.

Still another related object that should intrigue the collector of trivia is the novelty pencil sharpener, which came to maturity in the thirties and forties. Many of these were figurals, including representations of Charlie Chaplin, Popeye, Mickey Mouse, Charlie McCarthy, and also of such things as dogs and guns. Originally selling for a dollar or less, their values have started to rise and are destined to go higher still.

And for the absent-minded, there is the delightful shopping list or memo tablet, beloved by forgetful ladies of seventy-five to a hundred years ago. These miniature tablets had silver or decorated celluloid covers, some tied at the top by ribbons, others possessing a small ring by which they could be affixed to the person. Inside were writing leaves and a celluloid backing. These were the forerunners of today's memorandum pads and they were used by housewives to jot down chores and errands. Apparently few of these have been advertised for sale in recent years, but they are charming and those with silver covers will now be worth several dollars each. Undoubtedly some of these, perhaps with faded notations still on their pages, are languishing at the back of dresser drawers or elsewhere in the possessions of elderly folk.

Out in Farmington, Missouri, L. F. Brodsky has assembled what may be the world's most fascinating collection of typewriters, including models of some of the earliest ever produced. Mr. Brodsky and his wife, Jan, are among several collectors now seeking early makes of these machines whose commercial production goes back about a century when a fellow named Christopher Latham Sholes and an attorney, Carlos Glidden, were granted a patent for a device they called a "Type-Writer."

The Brodskys have been collecting what they term "mechanical Americana" for a decade, and they say that collecting typewriters "is just one of the avenues we travel to enlighten ourselves about the mores and divertissements of the past."

There are some fantastic machines in the Brodsky collection, including brands that are likely to be unfamiliar to today's generation, among them an 1884 Hammond; an 1887 Franklin; a Crandall of the 1880s; a Lambert, invented in 1896; a World, invented by John Becker in 1886; an Odell of 1889; a Blickensderfer, patented in 1892, and a Chicago, perfected in 1897 and differing from other wheel types in that its sleeve with type moves from side to side instead of up and down. They have several early wheel-type machines. The wheels containing the type for these were raised vertically by a number of methods to one of three or four levels, then twisted to line up the proper letter. The first of this type was the Crandall of 1879.

Memo tablets of 1900 with sterling-silver covers and celluloid leaves.

Their collection also boasts several miniature machines, including the Bennett and the Junior, invented by Charles A. Bennett in 1907 and 1910, respectively. These have a type wheel somewhat similar to that of the Blickensderfers. Typical of the "thrust forward" type of machine is their Wellington ⚹2, whose keys shoot straight out from a level plane in the manner of a snake striking.

There were numerous typewriters on the market late last century at prices of $5.00 or so that were guaranteed to work as well as those costing ten to twenty times as much. Among these were brands called Pearl and World Type-Writer. In the world of antiques early typewriters are still sleepers as are various other early business machines that forecasters say are going to be sought soon at much higher prices.

Speaking of prices, numerous early vintage fountain pens are selling at $1.00 to $2.00, but recently an engraved Waterman with sterling barrel was offered at $17.50, a 14-karat gold pen in a monogrammed case at $22.50, and a pen with a silver filigree case and eyedropper filler in the original box at $50!

Other values include:

Charlie Chaplin figural, metal, 1920s, made in Germany $12.00
Charlie McCarthy figural $6.00 to $12.00
Coca-Cola promotional $8.00
"Dandy" with last patent date 1919 $12.00
Dog's head figural $9.00
Mickey Mouse figural, plastic $5.00
Pistol figural $6.00
Popeye figural, 1929 $12.00
Standing flapper figural, made in Germany $7.00

TYPEWRITERS

Blickensderfer No. 5, patent date of 1892, with case $65.00 to $110.00
Blickensderfer No. 6 $35.00
Blickensderfer No. 7, with wooden case $25.00
Densmore No. 4, with metal cover $65.00
Fox, dated 1902, in tin case $17.00
Franklin, circular keyboard, *ca.* 1890 $80.00
Odell, 1889 patent date $17.50
Oliver No. 5, 1909, with original case $25.00
Oliver No. 3, 1898 $15.00
Oliver No. 9, last patent date 1914 $15.00 to $60.00
Smith Premier, double keyboard $35.00 to $50.00

PENNY ARCADE
DEVICES

THOSE WHO MISSED OUT on a visit to the so-called penny arcades that flourished earlier in this century missed one of life's joyous experiences. These parlors of mechanically operated machines that vended, for a penny, everything from one's fortune to flip views of scantily clad ladies flourished in the larger cities around the land and particularly in resort areas.

The machines of which we speak are the nongamblers in the sense that for each penny deposited they did yield some return as contrasted with such contraptions as the "one-arm bandits" and allied outlaws that gave the sucker only that small percentage of a winning chance that induced him to deposit his last copper and to borrow a few more from friends. These machines from counter-top to floor models are being collected today, but the focus is just now turning upon the nongambling vendors that dispensed such a tremendous variety of goods and "services" as, in addition to those just mentioned, perfumes, candies, gum, handkerchiefs, "art" poses, popcorn, and razor blades; there were also coin-demanding contrivances that purportedly enabled one to test his strength and lung power.

Interest is also awakening in large floor-model pinball games, large numbers of which are still around in much more sophisticated versions than their predecessors. The early ones primarily utilized steel balls that were propelled by a hand-operated plunger around a mazelike board, ending up in numbered pockets occasionally though not as frequently as they ended up in the trough that returned them to their starting point.

True, many, if not the majority, of the early pinball games were used for gambling, despite printed stickers or small signs on them that proclaimed to the contrary. Some dispensed coins in "secret" slots to winners; some dispensed merchandise to winners, and in the case of others players simply pitted their luck against one another for a small bet.

These machines of all types reached such popularity that miniature versions were produced for use in the home; but it is the larger commercial versions that

Pulver gum-vending machine with mechanical policeman.

are now wending their way into the homes of collectors. So, too, are the commercial machines that vended music via automatically played records.

The fact that devices of this type are heading toward maturity as collectors' items was attested to not long ago by an auction devoted to them and held by the internationally known Sotheby Parke Bernet Galleries. The galleries pointed out in their catalogue, incidentally, that these artifices of man's ingenuity (and his ineluctable longing to take a chance) actually date back to antiquity, among the earliest having been an urn in a temple in Alexandria in the first century A.D. that spurted water when a coin was dropped in the proper place.

Even punchboards of the type that put in their appearance half a century ago are starting to move into the collectors' market. Five dollars may seem a fancy price to pay for a decorated piece of cardboard filled with holes; yet that's what many punch boards are now bringing. The miscellaneous objects now being sought include even fortune card vending scales, especially now that we are becoming a nation of weight-watchers.

Some of the large floor-model gambling and vending machines with complicated mechanisms sell for rather high prices, but smaller models are available for sums that are small in comparison with what they will be bringing within a few years.

Here are some recent prices of both gambling and nongambling machines and a variety of other vendors and erstwhile penny arcade devices:

American Eagle slot machine, reel type, $.05 play $150.00
Bubblegum vendor, ca. 1938 $25.00
Candy mint dispenser, three tubes, $.01 slot $35.00
Caile-O-Scope, wooden table model $200.00
Card-vending machine, wooden, 6 feet high, $.01 slot $100.00
Challenger Target machine $75.00
Dice-a-Matic gambling machine, $.01 or $.05 play $125.00
Football gum machine, lever-operated with balls $45.00
Fortune-telling machine, floor model, 7 feet high $1,200.00
Fortune-telling scales $100.00
Gottleib Grip machine $40.00
Hockey game machine, early $200.00
Imp counter-top gambling machine, cigar-store type $55.00
Jacks, a large Mills gambling machine, $.05 play $200.00
Mills counter-top "one-arm bandit," wood and metal $175.00 to $250.00
Mills Windmill peanut vendor $200.00
Mills gum machine, small model $35.00
Movie machine, coin-operated, 16 mm., early $200.00
Mutoscope drop-card machine $200.00
Nickel-in-the-Slot cigar machine $135.00
Peanut dispenser, cast-iron base, glass ball top $50.00
Penny scales, cast iron $95.00
Photoscope $.01 metal stereoptic viewing machine with cards $175.00
Pinball machine, "Triggie Springless Automatic," wood, early $75.00

Pulver gum machine with clown $75.00 to 125.00

Pulver gum machine with policeman $125.00

Pick-a-Pack gambling machine with wheel and dice, wood, metal, and glass case
(cigarettes) $250.00

Puritan Baby Bell, fortune machine with reels $150.00

Robin Hood skill game machine, metal and glass, 20 inches tall $165.00

Round-a-Wheel cigar gambling machine, counter-top, *ca.* 1900 $150.00

Strength tester, floor model, 6½ feet high, cast-iron stand $375.00

Tickette vendor, blue metal, $.05 play $75.00

Trading card-gum vendor, $.01 slot $18.00

Win a Cigar machine, 23 inches tall, wooden spinning wheel, *ca.* 1900 $200.00

Win a Pack of Cigarettes machine, slot type, three reels $125.00

Zeno gum machine, yellow enamel, patented 1908, $.01 slot $45.00 to 60.00

PLAYING CARD CASES

PLAYING CARDS of one type or another date back centuries. Old Chinese records attribute their invention to the twelfth century A.D., and they are known to all civilized countries of the world and even to some fairly primitive cultures. Playing cards have also been collected for years, but the playing card case has received scant attention. Yet these containers are alluring in their own right and can truly be exciting to collect.

Decorated playing card cases have probably been neglected because so few collectors know about them, and this certainly is due in part to the fact that innumerable decks of cards and their original containers have become separated through the years. The containers have been made of sterling silver, electroplate, leather, ceramics, and boards.

Simpson, Hall, Miller & Company designed and produced some ornate chased-silver card cases in the form of footed stands about four inches high early in this century. The deck of cards was removed and reinserted through an opening in the top.

In 1892, Bloomingdale Brothers offered for $.67 cents an engraved silver-plated card case in book form with a clasp. Meriden Britannia Company turned out some silver-plated cases large enough to hold both a deck of cards and a set of poker chips. Depicted on the top of these cases was a "straight flush," accompanied by the lettering "A Fairly Good Hand." It was an expensive container —$16.88 wholesale.

Two-piece sterling-silver playing card cases with chased Art Nouveau decorations of sinuous form were made early in the century; the top half of the cases fitted over the bottom. At a time when Art Nouveau is again in the limelight, these cases will be of major interest.

Playing card cases of fine leather have been manufactured for about a century, some designed to hold a single deck, some two, and others for cards and poker chips, or bridge scorepads and pencils. There were also metal snap cases covered

Sterling-silver playing card case by Unger Brothers.

with simulated leather. Congress bridge cards some years ago were packaged in velour cases.

Even the lithographed light cardboard cases in which so many packs of cards were sold half a century ago offer a challenge to collectors because of the extraordinary variety of designs imprinted on them. These range from cupids riding bicycles to love birds, flowers, clowns, portraits, and scores of outdoors scenes.

All of the early playing card cases and boxes are worth seeking, although discriminating collectors are most likely to seek those of silver. The latter will be priced from $15 up. Leather and paper or cardboard cases will be much cheaper.

Early card games for children are also worth seeking, particularly if still housed in their original boxes and complete. Incomplete games are of little interest. Late

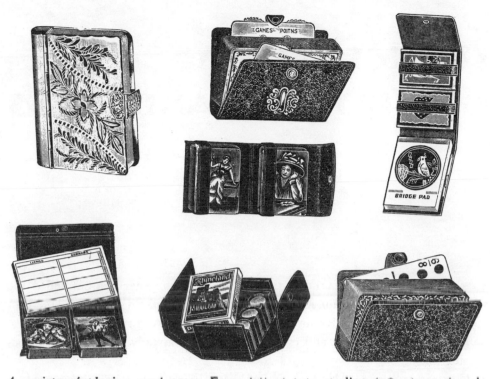

A variety of playing card cases. From left at top: sterling (1892); seal-grain leather with sterling ornament (1907); leather case of 1940. In center is a levant-grained leather case with two decks of cards (1917). Bottom row from left: box-shaped leather case (1918); case of seal leather (1918); black seal case (1907).

nineteenth- and early twentieth-century card games of this type are now available in a price range of about $2.50 to $15, depending largely on scarcity and the type of game.

For collectors there is a Playing Card Collector's Association, Inc., with chapters in various areas of the country.

PUMICE STONES, GRINDSTONES, AND RASPS

THE ELECTRICALLY OPERATED KNIFE and scissors sharpener has outmoded the whetstone, and the itinerant scissors grinder has disappeared from the American scene along with the peddler and his horse-drawn cart. As a result, pumice stones, hand-cranked grindstones, and even early rasps are already on their way to becoming antiques.

The pumice stone, a kind of porous volcanic glass, has long been used in powdered form as an abrasive; but probably not many of us are aware that small pumice stones, shaped and attached to silver handles, were used last century as manicure accessories. In addition to those with long handles, some were made with a silver cap and ring on one end by which they could be handled and hung. These were offered in shops along with nail scissors, buffers, and files at what today seems like an incredibly low price—$2.00 to $5.00, including the silver handle or cap.

Numerous types of abrasive materials were used in earlier years for sharpening everything from scythes to knives, and they were known by various names, including Washita stone, Hindostan oil stone, sandstone, Persian grit stone, corundum, and others. Mounted round grindstones operated by foot power were in widespread use up to the 1930s and some are still in use. Others were operated with a crank handle. But by the thirties belt power was largely replacing hand and foot power. These mounted stones saw yeoman service on farms all over the

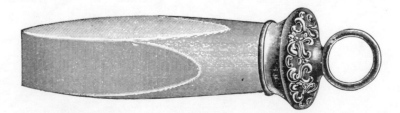

Pumice-stone manicure accessory with silver handle and ring, 1900.

130

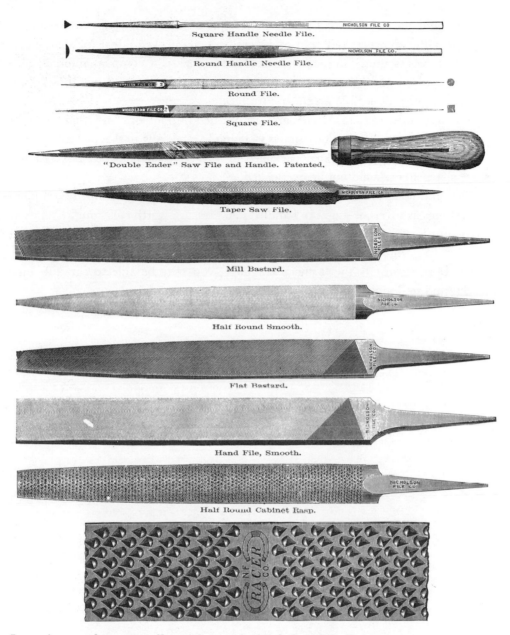

Square Handle Needle File.

Round Handle Needle File.

Round File.

Square File.

"Double Ender" Saw File and Handle. Patented.

Taper Saw File.

Mill Bastard.

Half Round Smooth.

Flat Bastard.

Hand File, Smooth.

Half Round Cabinet Rasp.

Late nineteenth-century files and rasps by Nicholson File Company.

country as well as in shops that needed them for the sharpening of tools and implements.

Also collectible are early tool grinders that were clamped to tabletops or workbenches and used emery wheels and other abrasives. There were special-purpose grinders, such as those intended to sharpen sickles and lawn-mower blades.

Numerous small oil and water stones were made for handling small sharpening jobs around the home. Small pocket hones about three inches long and made of Carborundum powder were sold in general stores and were ideal for sharpening pocket knives, scissors, and small tools. (Corundum is a common mineral, aluminum oxide, translucent varieties of which are used as abrasives; Carborundum is an abrasive produced in an electric furnace.)

Kitchen stones were made of coarse grit formed into a block and mounted on a base of hardwood. Flat, oblong stones were made especially to sharpen axes. Some of the smaller stones were sold packaged in attractive cherry-wood boxes. Early skate sharpeners should not be overlooked.

Files and rasps of numerous types are still in use, but early examples, including such things as silver- or staghorn handled nail files, are worth collecting.

By and large, the items mentioned in this chapter have not yet been collected on any scale, but some of them will still be found on farms, perhaps in storage there. If you can talk the farmer's language, you may be able to cart off some prizes, and undoubtedly at a price you can afford.

PARASOL AND UMBRELLA MARKERS

THERE ARE ARDENT COLLECTORS, particularly in England, of wine-bottle labels, which came into use when decanters made their advent. These silver labels, attached to a chain for suspension around the neck of the bottle and intended

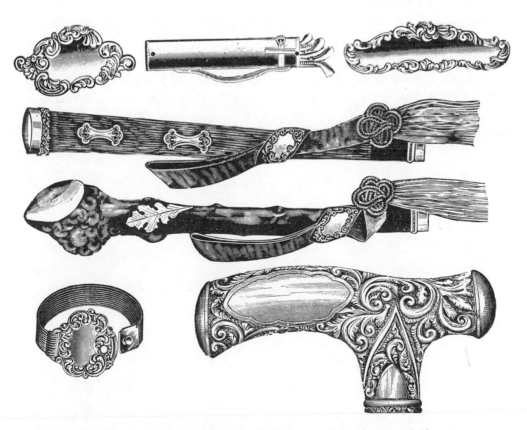

Silver parasol and umbrella markers, all dating early in the twentieth century.

to identify the contents, have been made since the mid-eighteenth century. There are also decorated wine labels of enamel and a few of porcelain. None of the wine labels are cheap.

A rather similar object, in wide use last century and early in this one, and one that should be just as collectible as wine labels though not as scarce as the early ones, seems not yet to have been "discovered" by the collecting fraternity. This is the parasol and umbrella marker.

The markers were small silver plates upon which one's name or initials could be engraved, and they were designed in quite a few shapes—oval, round, oblong, square—decorated by chasing or embossing in addition to engraving. Some were made with elastic bands that buckled to the marker itself and could be snapped around the umbrella handle; others were made to be permanently attached. There were also some that were attached with long ribbons with tassels on one end that imparted an air of elegance. Although the majority were sedate in appearance, some novelty ones were designed, including one in the shape of a miniature golf-club bag. Some of them could be used on either umbrellas or canes and were offered originally as "umbrella or cane markers." It is worth noting here that the handles of many umbrellas and canes were identical, since these two articles were frequently made by the same manufacturers.

The parasol and umbrella markers can be displayed by hanging them along a wall or housing them in small glass cases. Since collecting interest in them is due to be aroused soon but has been extremely limited thus far, they should be obtainable for a dollar or so, perhaps even less, and you can probably pick up some, complete with handsome parasols, at sales of old estates where you will find bidders so preoccupied with glass, china, and bric-a-brac in general that they ignore such lesser treasures.

POLICE AND FIREMEN'S BADGES AND ADJUNCTS

In Westwego, Louisiana, a young collector sits amid a shining array of badges that served long ago as emblems of authority and marks of public service and courage. These are police and fire badges in dozens of sizes and shapes that once decorated the caps or uniforms of law-enforcement and fire-fighting men all over the United States. There are badges designating all the ranks in police departments, badges once worn by sheriffs, deputies, marshals, and special police. There are badges in the shape of stars, oval badges, square badges, triangular badges, badges mounted with eagles, flags, fire-fighting paraphernalia, and other symbols. There are badges of tin, brass, bronze, and silver.

Bert Carbo has been collecting these badges for some time, and he expects to continue to seek them out for a long time to come. He started with a collection of the old badges of law-enforcement officers, then branched out into collecting firemen's badges and insignia.

The badges in his collection have come from around the country, many as a result of advertising for them. But he also has assembled a special collection of firemen's badges used in his home town. There are several other collectors with substantial quantities of the early badges—and there are likely to be more, because this field is wide open and challenging.

Although the emphasis here will be on badges, various other objects have moved into the category of law-enforcement collectibles, including such things as handcuffs, whistles, belt buckles, lanterns, patches, leg irons, and two newcomers—written criminal records, and mug shots of criminals. (Here a word of warning is in order. Mug shots are taken today of most persons arrested on felony charges before they are tried. Many defendants, of course, are acquitted of the charges against them, and one should be careful about displaying a photograph of an innocent person in a collection of photos of convicted criminals.)

Belt buckles and other insignia once used by self-appointed "vigilante" organizations are in great demand, and the buckles will bring as much as $50. One may

Police, sheriff, and marshal badges from the collection of Bert Carbo of West-wego, Louisiana.

also expect substantial prices for such other special insignia as badges of Indian police of the Apache Nation and the Texas Rangers.

Flashlights have long since outmoded the old bull's-eye police lanterns made of tole, and the latter, if in good condition and of a respectable age, will fetch substantially more than $25 on today's burgeoning market.

Fire-fighting adjuncts such as helmets, water buckets, uniforms, and fire-truck bells, as well as the related fire marks, have been collected for some years with values generally falling into a uniform range.

Nickel-plated (German silver) badges dating to the onset of this century or before are moving swiftly into the spotlight of collectibles. These include fire-hose company and engine-company badges, badges designating fire chiefs and assistant chiefs, and badges issued to special police, marshals, sheriffs, deputies sheriff, constables, and ranking officers from chief down.

Of greater interest and value are the specially designed police and fire badges of sterling silver or 14-karat gold with embossed designs of such objects as fire hoses, ladders, pumpers, and trucks or molded figures of eagles poised for flight. Although many stock badges were issued with lettered identification alone, or lettered identification plus a bit of engraved decoration, those of greater value bore on their surfaces depictions such as those mentioned above, and badges that bear the names of municipalities or counties are of greater value than those that do not.

(It may be of interest to note also that other types of badges of a century ago are now attracting collectors. These include those issued to newspaper reporters, hotel bellboys, express company agents, and railway employees. Of lesser interest are badges identifying members of such organizations as yacht and rifle clubs and fraternal bodies.)

Naturally, too, police revolvers are of prime interest as are holsters. Other things to watch for include firemen's watches, early uniform buttons, jail keys, and policemen's caps and helmets. And the latest addition to fire-fighter-related collectibles is the outmoded type of street fire-alarm box.

Here are some typical current prices:

Badge, constable, Highland County, Florida $10.00
Badge, deputy sheriff, six-pointed star, nickel silver $12.00
Badge, fireman's, New Jersey $4.00
Badge, fireman's, with eagle finial $3.50
Badge, fireman's, "Vigilant Hose—S.L.F.D.," pictorial, ca. 1890 $40.00
Badge, assistant fire chief $3.50
Badge, Indian Service Police, Apache Nation, ca. 1895–1910 $25.00
Badge, police, mid-nineteenth century, seven-pointed star, sterling $15.00
Badge, police captain, 1920 $15.00
Badge, special police (railroad), silver, late nineteenth century $25.00
Belt and holster, police $7.50
Billy, bird's-eye maple, ca. 1890 $10.00
Billy, fruitwood, 13 inches long $6.00
Cap, policeman's with visor, late nineteenth century $12.50
Criminal records with mug shots from police files, 1920s $2.00
Handcuffs, marked "Peerless," with key $35.00
Handcuffs, with screw key, ca. 1850 $22.50
Handcuffs, twentieth century $10.00
Helmet, police, brass finial, early twentieth century $17.50
Jail keys, various lengths, $1.50 to 8.00
Lanterns, bull's-eye, nineteenth century, tole $28.00 to 90.00
Leg irons with keys, nineteenth century $25.00 to 50.00
Texas Ranger belt buckle, plated silver $35.00
Vigilante (San Francisco) belt buckle, plated silver $50.00
Whistle, police, brass, nineteenth century $10.00 to 12.50

LETTER AND CARD RACKS AND HOLDERS

IN OUR FAMILY we have, for years, been filing letters and cards that need answering on desk and dresser tops, bedside tables, the television cabinet, a compote in the center of the dining table, and, occasionally, on the floor, where they cannot be overlooked.

But we have finally decided there is a better place: the old-fashioned letter and card holder—an inviting antique if there ever was one, and a utilitarian one to boot.

Card and letter racks. One at right on top row is silver-plated and other two are nickel-plated. The two at bottom, both silver-plated, were offered for sale in 1900.

The collector whose bank balance is ebbing will probably not want to start with Wave Crest letter holders, since the price of this ware has sprouted full-grown wings and has taken off into the wild blue yonder. If you insist on acquiring one, however, be prepared to shell out $165 to $225 for it.

Far less expensive but still delightful are other types dating from the 1880s through the early years of this century. Wave Crest, of course, is a glassware, and some other letter and card holders have been made of glass, but the majority were made of metal, usually either plated or sterling silver. They were variously termed post-card holders, letter-paper racks, paper and envelope racks, and desk racks, and they make most enticing decorative accessories for the home today. They are smaller than a bread box, which the double-decker modern office correspondence holder is not, but they are large enough to hold that assortment of post cards and letters that you have accumulated over the past few weeks and that you are going to get around to answering one day.

American silver manufacturers turned out some quite elegant designs, many featuring cut-out or open work, enriched with embossing and sometimes lettered. Some stood on round or scrolled feet, some on flat bases, and others were intended to be hung in some convenient place. There are letter and post-card holders with a relatively broad open space between the decorated back and front, others with several compartments, and some with a special compartment for stamps. There are also silver-plated post-card holders in the shape of a post card and intended to lie flat on a desk or table.

Though it is not quite cricket in these days of rampaging inflation to remind one of the good old days, we cannot resist pointing out that in the 1890s Bloomingdale's of New York offered an exceptionally handsome silver-plated letter rack with four compartments, an openwork front, measuring 5 inches wide by 4¾ inches high for the sum of $.47!

Silver and silver-plated ones usually cost more, however, prices of the former ranging from around $5 to $10 as this century opened. Of almost exactly the same type as letter and post-card holders were photograph stands, some of which were manufactured of metal and others of decorated celluloid sides and metal feet. Most of these had handles, but they, also, can be used for cards and letters.

One reason that these holders and racks are due for an increase in value is that interior designers are looking for small decorative objects for both apartments and homes, and these fill the bill admirably. Small boxes of all types are in the ascendancy at present. They are decorative, useful, and require little space. Among these, the silver and silver-plated stamp box of the 1890–1915 period was probably made in a greater diversity of designs and shapes than any other.

There are stamp boxes galore in the form of miniature match safes with hinged tops and embossed and engraved decorations, and there are flat and footed boxes quaintly engraved with such phrases as "I'm for Letters," "I'll Stick to You," and "U. S. Mail." There are also stamp boxes that are opened and shut with a

Novelty stamp boxes of the early 1900s. These are all of silver.

snap clasp and resemble miniature change purses, and about the turn of the century a group of oblong stamp boxes were fashioned in silver that doubled as court plaster (an early name for small adhesive pads for cuts) cases.

Silver and silver-plated boxes with Art Nouveau decoration caught the public fancy in the early years of this century, and these are charming. Letter and card holders of plated silver are available now in a price range of $15 to about $37.50, although one of Britannia metal embossed with cherubs and with separate compartments for letters and cards was recently tendered at $50. One of tin, advertising cocoa and featuring an illustration of children was tagged $20.

A few recent stamp-box prices include these:

Brass, hinged lid, three compartments $15.00
Enamel, brass feet, green with pink flowers, marked "China" $18.00
Enamel, maroon with blue flowers (Chinese) $18.00
Sterling silver, hinged top, embossed geometricals $15.00
Sterling silver, hinged top, Art Nouveau decoration $17.50
Silver plate, embossed decoration $7.50 to 15.00

MAGAZINES: SCIENCE FICTION, HORROR, AND ALLIED

THE GLAMOUR GIRL made her debut in the twenties, and these years and those following were the halcyon days of the glamour magazines and, ironically, of their very antithesis—the science fiction and the horror magazines. The latter grew up in the thirties and matured in the forties. The drugstore cowboy who whistled when the girls passed by and hoped fervently for a sudden breeze turned his attention during the moments unpropitious for girl-watching to thumbing the horror magazines on the drugstore racks, demonstrating that masculine weakness of vacillation between beauty and the beast.

These pulp periodicals devoted exclusively to tales of horror and the supernatural held the teen-ager spellbound, and they also did the same thing for his father, who read them somewhat more surreptitiously. Because they were printed chiefly on wood pulp, they were more susceptible to damage by wear and tear than the periodicals printed on more substantial enameled stock, and consequently large numbers were lost to posterity. Some of these magazines are still in existence, though not so many as there were two or three decades ago when they dealt with specters and wraiths, demons and ogres, harpies and sprites, the fiendish and the ghoulish, the incorporeal incorporated, the inconceivable conceived.

And then there are the early science fiction magazines, and these are about to be gobbled up by collectors, because so much of what once was fiction has now become fact. Rocket ships, laser beams, interplanetary travel—these and scores of other incredible figments of the minds of imaginative writers of a few decades ago have become reality today.

Many of the stories that appeared in the science fiction magazines were patterned upon those whose plots were originally conceived by such writers as H. G. Wells and Jules Verne, whose locales ranged from 20,000 leagues under the sea to the clouds.

In the science fiction and horror categories anything will be sought that relates the adventures of characters with such names as Captain Satan, Dr. Death, Dr.

Yen Sing, Red Hood, and Wu Fang, again to mention only a few among many. And, of course, there are the periodicals titled *Ghost Stories, Horror Stories, Marvel Tales,* and so on.

The pulps and the comics devoted to high adventure and detective fiction are also beginning to make a splash in those waters which the more venturesome collectors tread. Among those in this category that once cost cents but now bring dollars are *Aces, Air Stories, Air Trails, Black Book Detective, Dare Devil Aces, Federal Agent, Flyers, Jungle Stories, Racketeer Stories,* and *Sky Stories,* to mention just a few.

All of the early comic books are red-hot now, and prices of Volume 1, Number 1 of many are almost unbelievable so that the beginning collector might be better advised to start out with the regular monthly magazines, of which there have been so many in the areas we are writing about. Whereas old copies of such staid and once well-thumbed publications as *Ladies' Home Journal, Collier's, Woman's Home Companion,* and even the old *Saturday Evening Post* and others in their class, may bring a half dollar or a dollar (except for very early issues and those with special features such as cut-out paper dolls and the Brownies and other characters mentioned in a preceding chapter), the magazines devoted to science fiction, horror, and swashbuckling adventure will start at a dollar and go up to several dollars each.

Much interest is also awakening in the early-day movie magazines, especially in issues dealing with well-known screen personalities and the child stars and also those with "cheesecake" photographs that enabled the viewer to make eyeball appraisals of svelte or overstuffed female figures and muscular males. The movie books are now selling in a price range of $2.00 to $3.00 for the more commonplace ones and as much as $7.50 to $10.00 an issue for scarce early ones and those featuring cover photographs in color of stars who subsequently rose to great prominence in their profession. In great demand are magazines with photographic reproductions of the great stars of the silent film era.

None of these magazines is as plentiful today as one might think. They were discarded by the thousands when ennui set in; others have long since been recycled. To be salable, the magazines must be in first-class condition with covers intact and no missing or badly torn pages. There are a number of establishments around the country, including several in New York City, that specialize in back-number magazines. But one can often buy them more cheaply from individuals.

POSTERS OF
WORLD WAR I,
PRESS BOOKS, AND
MOVIE POSTERS

MUCH THE SAME TYPES OF COLLECTORS as those who seek the magazines mentioned in the preceding chapter are already on the lookout for World War I posters, movie press books, early theatrical bills or programs, and other paper materials issued prior to World War I.

Posters, in fact, are destined to experience something of a boom. Posters by such artists as Toulouse-Lautrec and other Art Nouveau era illustrators, including Eugène Grasset, Alphonse Mucha, Pierre Bonnard, Herbert McNair, and the Americans Will H. Bradley, Frank Hazenplug, and William Penfield, are for the collectors of status objects and, while highly desirable, are high in price in comparison with thousands of those done by lesser talent but which, nevertheless, merit perservation.

Circus and theatrical posters of early days have been of interest for some years but are beginning to move upward in value. This applies even to those issued three or four decades ago. Some fabulous posters were issued for Barnum and Bailey, Ringling Brothers, Forepaugh & Sells Brothers, John Robinson's Circus, and other great traveling shows. But some quite melodramatic ones also heralded the popular theatrical performances of several decades ago.

Movie posters are relatively recent arrivals on the collecting scene, and hundreds can be purchased at $10 or under. This is considerably less than prices being paid for quite early circus posters, although not many years ago these, too, were available for around $10. One well-known dealer in posters told me:

"Circus posters that we once sold for less than $10 now go for astronomical prices. We recently paid $150 for a two-sheet streamer depicting the complete 1894 Barnum and Bailey street parade, mounted on muslin. We sold it to a former movie director for $195."

Movie posters featuring stars prominent in silent films will often fetch considerably more than those of the talkie era, quite scarce ones being valued at more than $100. Into this bracket fall Valentino in almost any picture and Lon Chaney

Circus posters such as this early one appeal to young and old collectors alike.
Courtesy P. M. McClintock, *Franklin, Pennsylvania.*

in the memorable *The Phantom of the Opera*. But the good news for the collector is the fact that there is a tremendous difference in price asked from one dealer to another, for similar posters, many of the newer entrepreneurs in this field really having no idea as to whether there are established values or not, and the fact is that there are not.

There are, however, favorite types of posters, including those relating to horror films and movies of high adventure, and pictures of pin-up girls. Into the first of these categories fall films starring such actors as the late Lon Chaney and the late Boris Karloff and Bela Lugosi. The adventure films featured a host of stars; among them were Valentino, William S. Hart, Douglas Fairbanks, and Tom Mix. There were early "pin-ups" galore, among them Theda Bara, Clara Bow, Pola Negri, Dolores del Rio, and Jean Harlow. Highly collectible, too, are posters and other materials relating to Greta Garbo, Mary Pickford, John Barrymore,

John Gilbert, and such early comedians as Charlie Chaplin, Buster Keaton, Harold Lloyd, W. C. Fields, and Ben Turpin.

Posters appeal to younger collectors, some of whom use them for decorating entire walls of playrooms and dens or home bar areas. In fact, the decorative value of chromolithographed posters in the home has only recently been recognized.

Movie and stage-play programs rarely have this sort of decorative value, although they can be framed or displayed in cabinets; but their appeal is a nostalgic one, and a good many older persons collect them. They serve as mementos of memorable days of the past, tangible reminders of fun-filled hours.

Press kits are not so plentiful as posters and programs, because they were distributed originally to a limited audience, primarily newspaper and magazine critics. They contained photographs of the stars, scenes from the pictures, and mimeographed or printed background about the films and participants.

Movie star photographs have been collected by many persons over a number of years, but the press kits themselves are newcomers. You can buy them now for a dollar up, depending upon how elaborate they are and whether the picture in whose behalf they were issued became a smash hit.

World War I posters appeal to a fairly limited but growing audience. The most valuable are those drawn by noted illustrators such as Howard Chandler Christy, one of the creators of that enticing female we have come to know as "the American Girl," or Frederick Strothman, who gave us "Beat Back the Hun with Liberty Bonds." They include recruitment posters and those soliciting support for the Liberty Loan, War Savings stamps, the Red Cross, and so on.

Paper Americana of numerous types is just beginning to come into its own, and the values of those we have described in this chapter are going to move upward, probably very quickly.

Values of some of them include the following:

MOVIE POSTERS

Birthday Blues, starring the Little Rascals, 41×27 inches $6.00
Cocaine, adult film, 27×41 inches $36.00
The Corpse Vanishes, Bela Lugosi, 27×41 inches $17.75
The Eagle, Rudolph Valentino, 22×28 inches $110.00
Heart of New York, Al Jolson and Madge Evans, 27×41 inches $7.50
Outlaw Tamer, Lane Chandler, 26×40 inches $12.00
Road to Hollywood, Bing Crosby, 22×28 inches $4.00
Vampire Bat, Fay Wray, 26×40 inches $11.00

LOBBY POSTERS (CARDS)

The Eagle, Rudolph Valentino $20.00
Jaws of Steel, Rin Tin Tin $5.00

Early movie posters are now beginning to attract major attention. Courtesy
George Theofiles, *Baltimore, Maryland.*

London After Midnight, Lon Chaney $6.00
Loves of Carmen, Victor McLaglen $3.00

ENTERTAINMENT PROGRAMS

Circus, Barnum and Bailey's Greatest Show on Earth, 1930s $5.00
Circus, Cole Brothers, 1930s $5.00
Circus, Copper Whitby Circus & Tompkins Wild West, 1915 $7.50
Circus, Downie Bros., 1930s $10.00
Movie, *Fantasia,* 1940 $3.50
Movie, *Gone With the Wind,* undated $5.00
Stage play, *Last Days of Pompeii,* 1903 $7.50

PRESSBOOKS

Angels with Dirty Faces, James Cagney and Humphrey Bogart $5.00

Bar-C Mystery, The, Dorothy Phillips, 1926 $20.00

The Big Sleep $5.00

Breakfast at Tiffany's $4.50

Casablanca, Humphrey Bogart $5.25

A Bullet for Joey, Edward G. Robinson $6.50

Cinderella, a Walt Disney Production $7.00

Eagle of the Night, Frank Clarke, 1928 $10.00

Gunfight at OK Corral $6.50

Rockabye, Constance Bennett and Joel McCrea, 1932 $12.50

Room at the Top $5.00

Spitfire, Katharine Hepburn, 1933 $35.00

They Drive by Night, Humphrey Bogart $5.00

Thirty Seconds Over Tokyo $5.25

To Have and Have Not, Humphrey Bogart $5.50

Wild West, Jack Mulhall and Helen Ferguson, 1925 $15.00

WAR POSTERS

World War I, "Buy More Liberty Bonds" $20.00

World War I, "I Want You for U. S. Army" by James Montgomery Flagg $55.00

World War I, "Buy War Savings Stamps" $10.00

World War I, "Invest in the Liberty Loan" $10.00

World War I, Liberty Loan poster drawing by Howard Chandler Christy $40.00

World War I, Red Cross poster by Harrison Fisher $12.00

World War I, "We Belong to the Red Cross" $10.00

World War II, "Celebrate the 4th War Bonds" $7.50

World War II, "Four Freedoms" by Norman Rockwell $30.00

World War II, "Buy War Bonds" (Santa Claus illustration) $5.00

MUSTACHE COMBS
AND SILVER-PLATED
MUSTACHE CUPS

EIGHT YEARS AGO, a silver-plated mustache cup and saucer caught the fancy of R. L. McPeters of Hobbs, New Mexico, and he bought them. Mrs. McPeters was intrigued by her husband's acquisition—and today the McPeters have quite a collection: 101 silver-plated mustache cups and matching saucers that catch the rays of the morning sun and reflect them, mirrorlike, around the room in which they are housed.

Mr. and Mrs. McPeters were pioneers in the field of the metal cups and saucers at a time when other collectors were ignoring them for the ceramic ones, and now that hirsute appendages have made a smashing comeback, it might be appropriate to examine those silver-plated cups that kept grandfather from bathing his whiskers as he sipped his morning coffee three quarters of a century ago.

Interestingly, these were made in an even greater variety of designs than were those of ceramic. They are fully as utilitarian, and, since they have been neglected, they are still likely to constitute a bargain.

Until quite lately, in fact, plated wares have been outside the pale of discriminating collectors. But recent studies of silver-plated objects have begun to stimulate an interest in them. Not everyone can afford Georgian silver or the work of eighteenth-century American silversmiths but a great deal of plated silver is accessible even to those whose paltry wages have been frozen in our less than eminently successful efforts to combat inflation.

Many American silver manufacturers turned out these plated cups with their perforated metal guards on the drinking side and matching saucers between the waning years of the last century and about 1920. (Believe it or not, a good many ladies' mustache cups and saucers were made in the first decade of this century. There really weren't that many bearded ladies around, but mama had to have a cup and saucer that just matched papa's, so the sets were made for both male and female in the same patterns—except that mama's didn't have the mustache guard.) Many of the silver-plated cups and saucers were embellished with hand-engraved designs from arabesques to flowers. Some cups were gold-lined. Handles were fashioned in many shapes, the majority decorated by embossing.

Early in the century silver-plated mustache cup and saucer sets were wholesaling at prices of $3.25 to $5.80. Most were given heavier than normal coats of silver (triple-plated or quadruple-plated) since they were subjected to daily handling and wear.

Three turn-of-the-century silver-plated mustache cups and saucers and a lady's cup and saucer (bottom left), all gold-lined except one at bottom right.

Today's mustachioed male might also find the mustache comb of a century ago an aide in keeping his mustache neat. These, for the most part, were hinged to cases of plated silver, celluloid, or tortoise shell into which they folded so they could be carried about in the pocket; but there were also some without cases. (It may be of passing interest to note that some were referred to in whole-salers' catalogues as "bang or mustache" combs.) The silver-plated cases were decorated by embossing. The combs themselves were normally of celluloid or tortoise shell. Those with celluloid cases were quite inexpensive, but those with cases of silver plate sold for three or four dollars.

Since there has been almost no traffic to date in the silver-plated mustache cups and saucers or the combs, there are no fixed prices, but I've seen a few silver-plated cups in good condition at prices of $5.00 to $7.00, which is certainly below those for first-class ceramic ones. Others will cost up to $25. It will be more difficult to find cups with their original saucers, since the latter, after the popularity of mustache cups for daily use waned, were often pressed into service as pin trays and ashtrays. One should be able to obtain the combs for a dollar or two at most.

Collecting silver-plated mustache cups has an additional advantage for the beginner: they have not yet been reproduced, whereas those of ceramic are currently being reproduced in large quantities, and one will even encounter them where they have the least excuse for putting in an appearance—antiques shops and shows.

NEEDLE AND
THIMBLE CASES

THE ALMOST UNIVERSAL AVAILABILITY and convenience of store-bought textiles and the proliferation of organizations devoted to collecting used clothes (often when they're still new!) have combined to eliminate those once endless chores of mending and darning. This is rapidly relegating a host of home sewing accessories to the realm of the dodo and the dinosaur. Even now we find many of the tools and implements of the housewife preserved in museums and others flowing to the establishments of auctioneers who cater primarily to the purchasers of what the English term "furnishing antiques," which are those bought for household use and decoration instead of being relegated to display cases.

Pre-eminent among the small articles once indispensable in the sewing room are needle and thimble cases without which the housewife of yore might have searched through many a haystack in vain. And though these containers are small, they are by no means lowly.

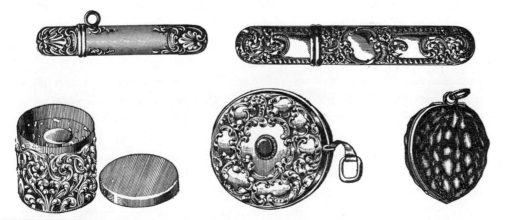

Sterling-silver needle cases (top), two thimble cases, and a tape measure (center), all ca. *1900.*

There is a difference between the needle case and the needle book. The latter was a sort of small booklet with pages of flannel into which needles could be stuck and readily found when needed. Some needle books themselves are desirable objects, largely because of their covers, which in some instances were made of mother-of-pearl and in others were of wood upon whose surfaces the home-grown artist occasionally exercised her talents.

The needle case was just that—a case in which to house needles so they would not become lost in a morass of socks that needed darning. There were tiny cases for sewing needles and larger ones for knitting needles. Very closely allied were cases for shuttles and for hairpins. Many of these cases made seventy-five to a hundred years ago are delightful, the more charming of them having been made of sterling silver with chased decoration, and other pleasing ones of horn, mother-of-pearl and wood. For those who could afford them, some cases were also made of gold and ivory. Ivory was particularly utilized for cases for knitting needles and hairpins, some with intricately carved decorations made in China and Japan. The nineteenth-century silver sewing-needle cases were usually fitted with a top attached to the case itself by a tiny chain to keep the two parts from becoming separated and misplaced. Many of the little sterling cases cost less than $2.00 each at the beginning of this century.

There were also some ingenious figural cases, including one in the shape of a walnut whose two halves snapped apart. A chain link was attached to one end of the case so it could conveniently be attached to a chatelaine. We have mentioned the chatelaine once or twice earlier in this book. This was a small device of silver or electroplate once worn at the waist. Some resembled large buckles with pierced openings, from which were suspended such articles as keys, other small household articles to which quick access was often needed, and even trinkets. The word is French and originally referred to the mistress of a castle or elegant household who carried on her belt or girdle cupboard keys, a purse, and other objects essential to her management of the estate. These buckles or clasps were revived in the late Victorian period and were used for both utilitarian and decorative articles, including keys, pencils, smelling-salts vials, small alarm whistles, needle and thimble cases, and the like.

In addition to the tiny cases we have mentioned, there were also larger combination cases intended to hold, for example, floss, needles, and thimbles, and even darning eggs. To find one of these with its original contents intact would be a matter of sheer luck.

And then there are the cases intended strictly for thimbles. Undoubtedly some of the collectors of thimbles also collect thimble cases, which are just as delightful as needle cases. Here again the choice ones are of sterling silver. Their basic shape is round, but the varied decoration of their exterior surfaces offers collectors quite a wide choice. The majority of those that will be encountered now stem from the late nineteenth and early twentieth centuries and feature pierced or openwork designs, although there are also solid cases with beautifully chased tops.

Although thimbles themselves are frequently written about in the collector periodicals and books, the cases are rarely mentioned, with the result that good collections of them are almost nonexistent, probably because so few persons realize how pleasant they are. This offers the collector an opportunity now to strike out in a field that is not already overcrowded and where "finds" may still be made.

Sterling-silver scissors, ca. *1900.*

There are various other sewing accessories that merit salvaging while there is yet time. Among these are figural embroidery scissors (those made in the form of a stork were heads-on favorites earlier); figural tape measures in decorated silver cases, (discussed in my *The Poor Man's Guide to Antique Collecting*); and even sewing machines themselves, which can be converted into "furnishing antiques" by home craftsmen. With the removal of the mechanism, those with drawers can be converted into dressing tables, and the fancy iron legs of others can be used to support a variety of small tabletops.

The value of needle and thimble cases will depend upon the material of which they are made, their age, and their scarcity. A wooden needle case originally issued as a souvenir of the 1904 St. Louis World's Fair is valued at $3.00; an earlier one with the original needles intact, $8.50, and a 4-inch-long case of carved ivory was recently priced at $20, which would be an excellent buy since the price of ivory is moving upward rapidly.

Values of scissors are similarly judged. A pair of German-made embroidery scissors with decorated handles is currently being offered at $5.00, and the same price is asked for a somewhat similar pair made in China. A pair of figural stork scissors has a $7.00 price tag, and a pair of sewing scissors with handles mounted with tortoise shell is advertised at $12.50.

Since sewing machines are not in demand at this writing, they constitute genuine sleepers for those interested. What few have been offered recently have brought between $5.00 and $25, except for very early ones with ornate iron legs, which have sold for more. You may have to bargain a bit, however, because some owners of the old machines apparently think their values should be comparable with those of baby grand pianos, failing to realize that no market has yet developed for them.

Here are some recent prices asked for tape measures:

Advertising, General Electric refrigerators $6.00
Advertising, Fab, 1919 $3.50
Advertising, Rose's Purity Rye whiskey, 1907 $12.50
Advertising, upholstering, celluloid case $3.50
Combination tape measure and pincushion with dog figural $8.00
Turtle figural, lettered "Pull my head, not my leg" $12.50

PLATES= CHILDREN'S PICTORIAL

ABC OR ALPHABET PLATES are a staple commodity in many antiques shops. They are great fun to collect, and their values are fairly stable. But not nearly so much attention has been given pictorial children's plates that are really in the same general category but lack the alphabet centers or borders.

These were made in quantity early this century in both ceramics and metals. Although these plates can occasionally be found in sterling, the majority were electroplated. To find silver-plated ones in fine condition will require a bit of searching since these plates were basically utilitarian and therefore subject to knife, fork, and spoon marks.

The original alphabet plates date back to the early nineteenth century, first made by the Staffordshire potters of England and shortly thereafter in the United States. The American pictorial nonalphabet plates did not appear in any quantity, apparently, until the late 1800s, but one finds many of them being offered in merchandise catalogues during the first two decades of this century.

Animal plates were favorites. These, along with a good many other pictorial plates, were sometimes produced as a part of boxed sets that also included a mug and a spoon—the three basic table necessities for small children. The Forbes Silver Company of Meriden, Connecticut, produced early this century such a set that must have pleased many children, showing a cat, its head and front paws emerging through foliage. Forbes also made a children's plate with Brownie-like creatures and a dog cavorting around the rim. Reed & Barton, of Taunton, Massachusetts, made a series of children's plates, bowls, and trays upon whose surfaces were engraved pictures of kittens, dogs, cows, horses, chickens, and other animals, as well as children, around 1920. The same firm produced children's trays with scenes from Mother Goose, Kate Greenaway figures, and teddy bears. A group of inexpensive nickel-plated plates featuring various animals in the bowl appeared around 1910 and sold at wholesale prices of only $8.00 a gross.

Nursery rhyme scene silver-plated plate with ABC cup and spoon by Homan Silver Plate Company, about 1914 (top); silver-plated ABC plate and pictorial cup by E. G. Webster, dating somewhat earlier.

Gold-lined oatmeal set, ca. *1917 (top); silver-plated pictorial plate of about the same date.*

Children's electroplated plates with nursery rhyme borders that included scenes from *Jack and Jill, Little Bo-Peep, Tom, Tom, the Piper's Son,* and others were favorites over a period of a number of years, beginning early in the century. These were made by Homan Silver Plate Company. Another favorite was a silver-plated set, the plate and mug of which were decorated with a scene of children in rowboats on a lake. Still another delightful silver-plated plate depicted a barnyard scene with two children and geese. The plate measured 7 inches in diameter and had an applied threaded border. There were also a number of pictorial electro- and silver-plated bowls and porringers. Outstanding among these was an oatmeal set, whose bowl was adorned with a series of embossed figures of children and was gold-lined inside. It was accompanied by an underplate. Porringers with their pierced handles appeared later, one of these with a rabbit engraved in its center appearing in catalogues dated as recently as 1940. These porringers were of sterling and measured 4½ inches in diameter.

The pictorial plates, bowls, and porringers should possess roughly the same values as do comparable alphabet plates, although since they do not yet have the following that the strictly ABC plates do, the collector may now be able to pick them up at lower prices. To give an idea of prevailing prices of alphabet plates the following list has been compiled from prices being asked as of this writing:

CERAMIC

5-inch diameter, January mythical scene in center $12.00
5-inch diameter, children playing in center (German) $18.50
5½-inch diameter, Franklin Maxim center $45.00
5½-inch diameter, man walking on stilts in center (English) $17.50
6-inch diameter, boy, woman, and dog in center $19.00
6-inch diameter, scene of girls washing clothes $18.50
7½-inch diameter, hunters and dogs scene in center $27.50
7¾-inch diameter, landing of Pilgrims in center $25.00
8-inch diameter, Little Bo-Peep in center $22.50

GLASS

6-inch diameter, clock face center $21.00
6½-inch diameter, girl's head in center $12.50
7-inch diameter, clock-face center, Vaseline glass $21.50
7½-inch diameter, Little Bo-Peep in center $24.50
No diameter given, marked "Clay's Crystal Works" $22.50 to 47.50

TIN

4⅛-inch diameter, Jumbo elephant center $22.50
7¾-inch diameter, *Who Killed Cock Robin?* center $29.00
8-inch diameter, *Mary Had a Little Lamb* center $25.00
8½-inch diameter, Palmer Cox Brownies scene in center $37.50

SILVER COIN HOLDERS AND SILVER WHISTLES

BACK IN THE DARK AGES when jitney bus fares were a nickel, a group of small silver coin holders appeared and were promptly referred to as "jitney coin purses." They were intended to hold small change, chiefly nickels and dimes. Nickels in those days would also buy almost any bottle of a soft drink, and for a dime one could sit through five showings of *The Perils of Pauline* at their favorite picture show.

Vanity cases of the same period frequently incorporated coin holders, but the individual holders with separate compartments for nickels and dimes were favored. They were made in round, oblong, and oval shapes. Some even had compartments for quarters to accommodate housewives who wanted to purchase such things as a pound of bacon or a box of stationery.

Most coin holders were made of either sterling or German (nickel) silver, and their sizes ranged from about 1½ inches in diameter to 3½ inches in length. Insofar as form was concerned, the majority of sterling-silver ones were relatively sedate, but some in German silver appeared in the shape of beetles,

Souvenir coin holders of the late nineteenth century.

159

clam shells, and crosses. Most came complete with attached chains measuring up to 50 inches in length.

Souvenir coin holders constitute a different but equally collectible category. These were intended to hold United States half dollars and souvenir coins, which were being collected at the outset of the century. The souvenir holders, all of round shape, were made of sterling silver, coin silver, 10-karat gold, rolled gold plate, and gold plate on a silver base. Those of 10-karat gold sold in 1900 for about $22.50 to $27.50. The other types were far less expensive and could be purchased at wholesale prices of $2.00 to $2.50 a dozen. Wearing souvenir coins on one's dress as a costume accessory was a practice of those days, and the little holders were fitted with a ring top by which they could be attached to the front of a shirtwaist or coat, serving a decorative fashion similar to that of a brooch. The souvenir holders put in an initial appearance at the time of the World's Columbian Exposition of 1893 in Chicago, and many were widely sold to house the Columbian half dollars associated with that celebration. A smaller size was made to accommodate the Queen Isabella souvenir coin or any quarters.

Since few things can be purchased for a nickel today and not many more for a dime, the "jitney" coin holders are moving into the classification of antiques, and the earliest souvenir coin holders are almost as desirable as the souvenir coins themselves.

Tiny silver whistles attached to the person by chains and often incorporated into the trappings of the chatelaines mentioned earlier were a very useful affectation in the 1890s and into the twentieth century. These little whistles measured only an inch or two in length but, when blown, emitted a shrill sound that could be heard for some distance. They were of particular value to women who were accosted by strangers on dark streets who used them to summon a policeman. It is reported, without confirmation, that they were also useful in summoning dogs and recalcitrant husbands. Chiefly, however, they were decorative little objects, worn in much the same manner as charms.

For such small articles, some were quite costly. One of plain satin sterling illustrated in an 1898 catalogue of the S. F. Myers Company of New York City cost $20 wholesale. But by 1900 there were ornately decorated sterling whistles that could be had for as little as $2.00 retail. Gold-filled ones sold for about the same price. Some of the silver whistles were created in whimsical shapes and are quite appealing. One was fashioned in the shape of a dog's head with a ring (to which the chain was fastened) attached to the animal's nose. There were others in the form of horses' heads and human heads.

A collection of coin holders or silver whistles would be ideal for the apartment dweller with cramped quarters who would like to pursue objects small enough to display in a limited area but of enough diversity to make their pursuit a challenge. Here again are objects that have appeared insufficiently in the marketplace to establish guidelines to their values, but many are almost certainly

Sterling-silver whistles, ca. *1900.*

still in the possession of their original owners or their families. The silver coin holders can probably be found for a few dollars each; the figural silver whistles will certainly come higher. However, one dealer very recently offered a silver coin holder for nickels, dimes, and quarters at $37.50, so if this field is of interest, you'd better get moving.

SOAPSTONE CARVINGS

REMEMBER WHAT HAS HAPPENED to those mud-colored pieces of plaster of paris statuary called John Rogers Groups? They have soared in value from their original prices of $10–$25 to a range of $225 to $350, and there are far more buyers than sellers.

The same thing may happen to those carved soapstone groups that one encounters in scores of antiques shops and at most antiques shows at prices representing a fraction of those asked for the Rogers Groups. We are not talking here of the inconsequential match holders or little monkey groups symbolizing the maxim "Speak no evil, see no evil, hear no evil," but rather of more substantial carvings executed with obvious skill on that massive variety of talc with the greasy feel.

American soapstone, found primarily in western North Carolina and Virginia, is used mainly for utilitarian purposes. Although some carvings have been made in the United States, the finest ones come from China and Japan, where artisans have carved soapstone into a great variety of ornamental objects. Many of the so-called Chinese soapstone carvings, however, are actually made from agalmatolite, sometimes called pagodite or figure stone, or from pyrophyllite, much of which is also found in the United States. Agalmatolite is a gray or green stone, relatively soft and often streaked with other colors. In addition to being easy to carve, it takes on a sheen when polished. Pyrophyllite, like soapstone, has a greasy feel and is sometimes called pencil stone.

Soapstone is not difficult to carve. The mineral is soft but relatively durable and, in addition to carved ornaments and groups, it has been utilized in the past for such things as hearths, tubs, and tabletops. It is found in various colors ranging from gray to purple-brown.

The carvings evidence varying degrees of skill, and the reason that the majority of them remain inexpensive is that connoisseurs have avoided them like the plague and other collectors haven't taken the trouble to attempt to differentiate between the crude carvings turned out quickly for the hoi polloi and those done by adroit artists who took their work no less seriously than did those who sculpted in bronze or marble.

Some carved soapstone groups are fairly large but the majority seem to be under 10 inches in length. Many boast intricate detail: figures, flowers, leaves, birds, and a variety of incised decorations. Many were intended as containers for such small flowers as violets. Monkeys were favorite figures, and one will encounter them in amusing poses, reflecting the sculptor's sense of humor, as well as his understanding of the monkey's habits. The backs of these carved groups were usually left flat in much the same manner as the Victorian flatback chimney ornaments.

With bronzes and stone sculptures selling in the hundreds and, frequently, thousands of dollars and even with contemporary metal and glass sculpture bringing some fantastic prices, collectors on limited budgets are probably going to recognize very soon the merits of some carved soapstone groups, relatively few of which are now bringing much over $60.

A part-time antiques shop operator in the small but historic town of Roswell, Georgia, who travels around the country during the week and keeps shop on weekends, has been picking up the better examples of soapstone carvings at antiques shops in the cities he visits. He doesn't sell them: he's building a collection. But one day, and probably quite soon, he's going to have a small fortune on his hands—if he decides to sell them during that inevitable time when the market will rise.

Meanwhile, if the prospect interests you, try to locate some of the better examples at such prices as the following:

Basket with carved monkeys, bats, and flowers, gray and cream, 8×9 inches $50.00
Bookends, carved mountains, trees, houses, 4×5 inches $25.00
Bottle, carved Chinese "Immortals," white $40.00
Elephant, small $18.00
Figure, carved oriental figure on pedestal, 5 inches high $20.00
"Foo" dog, small $11.00
God figure, black and brown, 4 inches high $20.00
Inkwell, carved on two sides $22.00
Urn, carved dogs and flowers, rose-brown, 7×5½ inches $22.00
Vase, carved flowers, 10 inches high $35.00
Vases, carved with profusion of flowers and birds, 12 inches long, 9 inches high, 4 inches wide, pair $125.00
Water buffalo in reclining position, 3¼ inches long $25.00

MEMENTOS OF SPACE EXPLORATION

FOR ALL HIS JUMPING OVER BUILDINGS at a single bound, Superman never made it to the moon. But American astronauts have, and a new class of highly collectible objects has thereby been created. Anything and everything relating to the exploration of outer space is now attracting both dedicated collectors and speculators. Since it is obvious that no tangible objects from outer space, such as rock samples from the moon, can be bruited about in the marketplace— at least not yet—the concentration is primarily upon ephemera. This includes autograph letters and signatures of the astronauts, their photographs, songs relating to their achievements, drawings, and first-day stamp cancels signed by the astronauts.

It follows logically, since so many enterprising Americans are eager to turn over a quick buck, that our exploits in space have been capitalized upon by a number of small and hastily set-up manufacturing plants, some established in basements of private residences, and the result is a plethora of cheap souvenirs, some offered at exorbitant prices. The cautious collector will look at these closely before plunking down cold cash.

Figural bottle-makers were among the first to devise and put on the market mementos of space exploration. Your guess as to the future of these is as good as mine, but it should be noted that the craze for brand-new figural bottles has shown an abrupt slackening of late and prices of many have fallen drastically. One ceramic bottle commemorating the Apollo flight and intended to hold a liquid is said to have been rejected by the government because it displayed a United States flag. The producers then tendered the empty container at $15 with an offer to throw in the label originally intended for it for a quarter extra, "for collecting purposes only." Commemorative plate producers also have entered the fray, and right now some commemorative plates are red-hot on the market. Whether and when the flame will die is also anybody's guess. (It may be pertinent to add here that plates are now being turned out to commemorate Christmas,

Mother's Day, Father's Day, the Olympics, Thanksgiving, Easter, the Pope, old master painters, the late President Kennedy, the late Dr. Martin Luther King, the landing of the Pilgrims, Whistler's Mother, and Uncle Sam, in addition to the Apollo flights and the moon landings.)

Caricatures and portraits of the astronauts and comic drawings relating to the moon landings are among the mementos being sought. Song sheets with pictorial covers that include such scenes as John Glenn's space capsule in the ocean are bringing a very few dollars now but are apt to be selling higher even by the time you finish this book. The same is true of various photographs, especially those showing the moon's surface and space capsules.

Typed copies of manuscripts signed by one or more astronauts will now bring higher prices if they pertain specifically to either the space flights or incidents in the lives of the astronauts. Those with multiple signatures will naturally bring the highest prices.

Prayers broadcast from Apollo 8 from orbit have been printed on parchments and, accompanied by Apollo 8 stamps with first-day cancels, already are bringing good prices, and especially if they are also autographed by any of the astronauts or other leading figures associated with the space program.

Before this country's space program slackens, we may expect numerous additional objects relating to the achievements to wend their way to market; but those likely to appreciate most in the future are those issued in limited quantities, and those issued earliest.

Here are some current values:

AUTOGRAPHS

Buzz Aldrin, Richard Truly, and Joe Allen signatures on cover dated Jan. 19, 1965 $25.00

Apollo 15 tracking station cover signed by Buzz Aldrin and Ed Gibson, dated July 27, 1971, plus GTA-10 recovery ship cover signed by Aldrin and "Shorty" Powers, July 22, 1966 $45.00

Apollo 14, three covers signed by Bob Overmeyer, Deke Slayton, Joe Engle, Gordon Cooper, Bob Crippen, Joe Allen, Richard Truly, Eugene F. Wigner, and Admiral David McDonald $35.00

Cosmonauts A. G. Nikolayev and Vitaly I. Sevastyanov signatures on Soviet cover commemorating flight of Soyez IX, June, 1970 $50.00

Michael Collins signature on 1967 twin space-plate block first-day cover $30.00

Edward H. White (died in Apollo project) signature on FDC Project Mercury stamp, dated "Cape Canaveral, Feb. 20, 1962" and inscribed to a friend $50.00

Three first-day covers, Project Mercury stamp and cancel, signed by Neil Armstrong, Charles Conrad, Jr., and Alan B. Shepard, dated "Cape Canaveral, Feb. 20, 1962" $85.00

Apollo Mexico cover signed by James McDivitt, Edward G. Gibson, Deke Slayton, Richard Truly, and David Holmquist $22.50

PICTORIAL MATERIAL

Alan Bean caricature, original, by Jack Rosen, 7×10 inches, signed by Bean with a machine signature $25.00

Richard Gordon, Jr., caricature, original, by Jack Rosen, 8×11 inches, signed by Gordon by hand and machine $25.00

MISCELLANEOUS TYPED AND PRINTED MATERIALS

Biographical sketch (2 pp.) of Herman Oberth typed on parchment with Moon Landing stamp and first-day cancel at top of first page $12.50

Account of Apollo 12 mission by Charles Conrad, typed on parchment-type paper, 4 pp., signed at end by Conrad $100.00

Typed manuscript, "A Chance for Immortality," by Scott Carpenter, 10 pp. containing his pre-astronaut adventures, etc. $30.00

Printing of prayers broadcast by Apollo 8 from orbit by Mike Collins with Apollo 8 stamp with first-day cancel $40.00

Printing of "Prayer from Lunar Orbit" signed by Alan B. Shepard, Jr., and Stuart Roosa with first-day cancel of Apollo 8 stamp $50.00

PHOTOGRAPHS

Alan B. Shepard, Jr., and other Mercury astronauts at White House with President Kennedy and Vice President Johnson, 8×10 inches, with first-day cancel of JFK stamp with combined Mercury stamp, signed by Shepard $50.00

John Glenn with President Kennedy, Wernher von Braun, and others with first-day cancel of JFK stamp, signed by Glenn and James E. Webb $30.00

SHEET MUSIC

"The Biggest Ride Since Paul Revere, the Ballad of John Glenn," with photo of Colonel Glenn on cover, published in 1962 $3.75

"American Moon" (relating to Apollo 8), with illustration of United States flag and man in the moon, published in 1969 $3.00

"Everyone's Gone to the Moon," with photos of Apollo 11 astronauts on moon's surface and of President Kennedy, published in 1969 $3.00

"The Flight of Friendship 7," with photograph of John Glenn's spaceship in water, published in 1962 $3.25

"One Small Step," with color photograph of astronaut on moon's surface, published in 1969 $3.00

STAINED-GLASS WINDOWS

STAINED GLASS goes back a good many centuries, first having been utilized for ecclesiastical purposes in the sixth century by the Byzantines. During the medieval period a ruby-colored stained glass was obtained by adding copper to the glass batch. Magnificent church and cathedral windows still extant in Europe attest to the skills of the stained-glass window-makers. We are not concerned here, however, with the huge stained-glass windows of the Middles Ages, although this subject is a fascinating one, but with those much smaller windows that decorated thousands of Victorian era homes in this country and abroad.

These windows were utilized in various rooms of the home, frequently for the glass portion of the main entrance door and often in those sedate rooms, reserved primarily for company, called parlors. Although these windows did not compare in dimensions with those in the magnificent cathedrals, they nevertheless were, for the most part, considerably larger than the windows in American homes of the twenties through the forties. Smaller windows were often used in bathrooms, however.

Early in this century, the talented Louis Comfort Tiffany produced some beautiful Favrile glass windows that were opalescent and iridescent and differed from the traditional stained-glass type then in use. The advertising department of Tiffany Studios issued in 1913 a handsome brochure devoted to the products of the company's Ecclesiastical Department in which it bestowed some extravagant praise on these windows. The basic material for them, the brochure claimed, "surpasses the best of the medieval glass workers, whose art reached its zenith in the thirteenth century. The glass alone would make these windows distinctive, but in design Tiffany windows possess individuality. There is no radical departure from what may be called the conventional, and there is no attempt to copy anything but the spirit of the best work of the Middle Ages; nevertheless, Tiffany windows are wont to be considered as easily distinguishable from other windows, as the work of the renowned Corot is differentiated from that of his would-be imitators."

Leaded glass window in various colors, obviously influenced by the Art Nouveau movement. From the author's collection.

The colors were obtained by gradations in the glass, and no paints, stains, or enamels were used. The brochure added:

"The Favrile glass is so rich in color combinations it lends itself to the most comprehensive designs involving figures and landscapes. Many designers of ecclesiastical architecture in America, who have made a careful comparative study of the properties of colored glass with especial reference to Tiffany Favrile glass, have pronounced as faddists those architects who resort to imported painted glass for church memorial or decorative windows."

Tiffany windows, truly majestic, were installed in many churches and other structures in this country, including the Church of the Messiah, Brooklyn; the Russell Sage Memorial Church Building of the First Presbyterian Church, Far Rockaway, New York; St. Paul's Church, Paterson, New Jersey; the Masonic

LEADED ART GLASS.

2449. $0.00 per sq. ft

2450. $7.40 per sq. ft.

2452 $8.00 per sq. ft.

2451. $9.60 per sq. ft.

2453. $8.60 per sq. ft.

These leaded and stained-glass windows made by the Hafner Manufacturing Company of St. Louis in 1908 are in the Art Nouveau style.

169

Chapel, Utica, New York; the Public Library, Winchester, Massachusetts; the residence of R. B. Mellon, Pittsburgh; the home of Captain J. R. De Lanar, New York City, and many others. They are out of the reach of most collectors of trivial objects, but numerous other windows of stained and leaded glass can be purchased at lower prices, though they are now rising. The fact is that a rush for these windows is now starting, and they are being installed in homes large and small to lend interest and color to both exterior and interior appearance.

The Wrecking Bar, an Atlanta institution that deals exclusively in architectural antiques, says the demand for stained-glass windows of all sizes is definitely on the upsurge and that prices have begun going up. The company told me that the greatest use of the windows currently seems to be for bathrooms. These windows usually range from 2×2 to 2×3 feet in size. However, larger windows are being used elsewhere in the home, including stairway landings, the company reported.

Small windows may occasionally be found for about $50, but the general current price range, depending on size and the excellence of the work, is from $75 to $200 with some exceptionally fine windows bringing as much as $350. These prices represent those being asked for stained-glass windows from American Victorian homes and from Europe and do not include the really extraordinary windows with extremely elaborate work, which will cost more.

Tiffany was not the only producer of fine opalescent glass windows in this country. The artist John LaFarge was also a pioneer in this field and produced some beautiful windows after much experimentation. He obtained drapery effects by squeezing the glass into folds or wrinkles while it was still molten. The only enameled part of his windows were the faces, hands, and hair of figures. One of LaFarge's windows was awarded the Legion of Honor at the French Exhibition of 1899. Other American stained-glass craftsmen included Lawrence Saint, Payne Spiers, and Charles Connick.

Early in this century when stained-glass windows were at the peak of their popularity, many persons who could not afford large pictorial windows used the colored glass to trim the edges of clear glass windows or doors.

Because of their fragility, panes have been broken in many of these windows from older homes and businesses. However, modern stained glass is being made, and broken panes can be replaced or repaired so that these damaged windows no longer need be considered a loss.

Most windows of this type now available date from the 1880s to as late as 1930. A decade or so ago, wrecking companies could hardly give them away, but these late Victorian pieces have now become modern Cinderellas.

TEAPOTS AND
TEAKETTLES

TEAPOTS AND TEAKETTLES have successfully courted the favor of collectors for years, and the old five o'clock teakettle is no exception. In gleaming polished brass, decorated electroplated Britannia metal, or copper, supported upon or held by a handsome stand of wrought iron or nickel silver, this kettle—named, of course, for the favorite tea hour—overshadows the starkly functional modern version no matter how mellifluously the latter may whistle.

Five o'clock teakettles were heated by small lamps that burned alcohol and there is no reason why canned heat cannot be substituted for the old burners to assure safe and smokeless operation. They were designed in numerous shapes and sizes, with short straight spouts or longer curved ones, and with metal or wooden handles. Their wrought-iron stands were made in almost endless variety. Some were attached by frames on their sides to bases supported upon tiny but sturdy feet. Some legs of twisted iron extended from the sides of the kettle down to the tabletop. And there were charming stands of twisted iron from which the kettles were suspended, the burners attached firmly to the bottoms of the stands. There were also stands of polished brass and nickel, some ending in paw feet, some in claw-and-ball feet. John Round & Sons of Sheffield, England, made some extravagantly decorated kettles of silver plate on Britannia metal with capacities ranging up to six pints. Electroplate or not, these were handsome enough to grace the finest table.

The smallest size made by Round seems to have been four gills, a gill being equivalent to half a pint. Included in its output was an oval kettle with a very high handle that sat upon a trivet-type stand of nickel silver and was decorated with swags and teardrops. Capacities of the American-made kettles ranged on the average from two to two and one-half pints. Including the stand, they stood about 11 to 15 inches tall.

Since readily available canned fuel can be used to heat the kettles, missing oil burners on the antique ones is by no means a calamity.

Five o'clock teakettles, ca. 1900. All of polished brass: one at bottom right has wrought-iron stand.

At the opening of this century they were offered in a wholesale price range of $3.13 to $12, which put their retail prices well within the means of all who observed the agreeable and refreshing custom of serving afternoon tea.

The price of the five o'clock kettles with stands should be a little above that for brass kettles of comparable age without stands and burners, but lower than that for teakettles that date back to the eighteenth or early nineteenth centuries. A very few have been offered for sale recently at prices of $25 to $40, complete with stands and burners.

For purposes of comparison, here are some recent prices of various types of teakettles:

Brass, amber handle, button feet $45.00

Brass, 10 inches high with hinged lid, very early $75.00

Brass, on stand with alcohol burner (five o'clock) $36.50

Copper, tilting, on brass and copper stand, 12 inches high including stand, cleaned and burnished $75.00

Copper, oval, 13 inches high, 17 inches long, wooden handle, early $95.00

Copper, three-legged, iron handle $52.50

Copper, gooseneck spout, 2-liter capacity $15.00

Copper, 10 inches high, 8½ inches in diameter, early $50.00

Copper, fancy brass and wood handle, ornate design, 5 inches high, made in China $25.00

Copper, gooseneck spout, brass lid, 1½-pint capacity, made in Holland $25.00

Iron, gooseneck spout, high dome $35.00

TEDDY BEARS

IF YOU THINK the recent rises in doll prices have been phenomenal, watch what happens to those of teddy bears in the next few years. The name given these stuffed replicas of bear cubs derives from the nickname of our twenty-fifth President, Theodore Roosevelt. There is a well-told story about a hunting trip taken by President Roosevelt during which he refused to shoot a bear cub because of its small size. This story is referred to in an excellent two-part article in the June and July 1972 issues of *Spinning Wheel* by Julie and Linda Masterson and is also told in the April 1972 issue of *Collector's World* by Stephanie Cooper Shulsinger. Mrs. Shulsinger says that Roosevelt made the trip in an effort to settle a boundary dispute between Louisiana and Mississippi and that the incident became the subject of a highly publicized cartoon by Clifford Berryman in the Washington *Star*. The cartoon, captioned "Drawing the Line in Mississippi," depicted Teddy Roosevelt, rifle in hand, declining to shoot the frightened bear cub.

The plush teddy bear became an almost overnight smash. Mrs. Shulsinger credits Morris Mitchom, Brooklyn toy-maker, with being the first to capitalize on the incident by obtaining permission from President Roosevelt to name his stuffed animals "Teddy." This venture subsequently developed into one of the country's largest toy producers, Ideal Toy Company.

From that day to this, teddy bears have been children's favorites. They've been made in all sizes from quite tiny to huge animals often given in recent years as prizes at fairs and carnivals. And they've been made in all colors, including many that bears themselves have probably never seen. There have been undressed bears (bare bears) and dressed bears; bears with glass eyes; bears on wheels; bears that doubled as muffs; bears with electric flashing eyes, and bears with devices simulating voice boxes. With the exception of the stroller bears and such novelties as muffs, the teddy bears had movable legs and frequently had eyes with rolling pupils. Many were dressed in clothes of percale and

Teddy bear named "Toby" with voice box in tail, 1920s.

other materials, complete to shoes and handkerchiefs. Some were equipped with walking mechanisms.

Eighteen-inch-tall teddy bears were wholesaling for as little as $16 a dozen in 1941. In the same year honey bears equipped with Swiss clockwork musical chimes and covered with lambskin wholesaled at $12.70 a pair (mama and papa). Brown plush teddy bears 4½ inches high could be bought for $1.70 a dozen.

With the prices of dolls—even those from the thirties, forties, and fifties—at an all-time peak, stuffed teddy bears are now destined to come into their own. The best place to buy them now is at garage sales when parents not yet hip to this coming craze offer them along with other playthings of now-grown children for a pittance, or in second-hand merchandise stores or such establishments as the Good Will Industries. If you don't know the bears' past histories, you'd better play safe and somehow disinfect them.

Since collecting them is really just ready to begin, it would be meaningless to

Frank Buck growling bear (top left); panda bears (top right and bottom left); honey bear.

list prices, but you should be able to pick up many for a very few dollars. Plush ones about forty years old are bringing $12 to $25 now.

The articles mentioned at the outset of this chapter are recommended to those who want to know more of the history of the teddy bear.

CENTENNIALS
AND EXPOSITIONS

A SMALL GLASS FIGURE OF ABRAHAM LINCOLN made by the glasshouse of Gillinder & Sons and originally sold as a souvenir will fetch $250 on today's collector's market. This figure is one of thousands of trivial objects produced as mementos of the Philadelphia Centennial Exposition of 1876.

The spirit of 1776 is due for another awakening when this country celebrates the bicentennial of its independence in 1976, and a frantic search for memorabilia, no matter how slight, of the celebration in Philadelphia a century ago has been under way for several years and is now reaching fever pitch, for many of these articles will be legitimate antiques very soon.

But the forthcoming observance has had a wider impact than focusing attention on the centennial: it has served to stimulate an interest in memorabilia of numerous other major expositions, and thousands of objects associated with these will also soon be in great demand so that right now is the time to look for them. Although a large percentage of the souvenirs fall into the class of trivia, numerous others have in fact become primary collectibles, among these being coins, medals, and objects made of glass and ceramics.

The scope of the Philadelphia Centennial is reflected in the fact that almost nine million people viewed at least a part of the 30,000 exhibitions during a period of six months and paid half a dollar each to do so. And this was in spite of the fact that the exposition was completely devoid of girlie shows or other sideshow attractions such as those that enlivened the Chicago Century of Progress Exposition that opened in 1933 and the New York World's Fair with its gala opening on April 30, 1939.

Several of the nation's most famous glasshouses had displays at Philadelphia's Fairmont Park a century ago, including the Boston and Sandwich Works, the New England Glass Company, and Gillinder & Sons. The last-named set up an operating glasshouse on the grounds and produced items that were offered for sale to the visitors. These pieces are among the most collectible of the Cen-

Wedgwood pitcher showing Memorial Hall at the Philadelphia Centennial.
Courtesy Stan Gores.

tennial Exposition souvenirs. Sold in profusion were such glass articles as paper-weights, bread trays, canes, bowls, plates, creamers and other pitchers, and goblets. Similar objects were made of pottery and porcelain and bore depictions of the famous Liberty Bell and other symbols of the war for independence or of buildings on the exposition grounds. Thousands of other objects were made of brass, copper, and other metals, wood, textiles, and other substances, and virtually every one is now collectible.

178

Although the focus is now on the Philadelphia Bicentennial, astute collectors will look toward the abundance of materials associated with other noted expositions, both in this country and abroad. Foremost among the expositions held in the United States were the World's Columbian Exposition, Chicago (1893); Pan-American Exposition, Buffalo (1901); Louisiana Purchase Exposition, St. Louis (1904); Alaska-Yukon-Pacific Exposition, Seattle (1909); Panama-Pacific International Exposition, San Francisco (1915); Sesquicentennial Exposition, Philadelphia (1926); Golden Gate International Exposition, San Francisco (1939), and the Chicago and New York fairs mentioned above.

There were various other expositions, all of which generated objects now collectible. These included the New York World's Fair at the Crystal Palace (1853), the Cotton States Exposition in Atlanta (1875), Trans-Mississippi International Exposition in Omaha (1878), Lewis and Clark Centennial Exposition in Portland (1905), Jamestown Tercentenary Exposition in Jamestown, Virginia (1907); Panama-California Exposition in San Diego (1915), and others.

Souvenirs of all of these fairs and expositions are multitudinous, including such a miscellany as post cards, brochures, first-day stamp covers, buttons, photographs, handkerchiefs, letter openers, ashtrays, clocks, games, lighting devices, pencil sharpeners, posters, clothing, jewelry, and silverware, to mention a few. Naturally

This metal tray is a Pan-American Exposition souvenir. Courtesy Bill Poese.

those stemming from the more recent observances are more abundant and, for the most part, less expensive than those from the early major celebrations.

We will not be concerned here with mementos of the more recent fairs except to point out that the collectors of these are increasing in number. Here are some values of typical collectible objects stemming from the earlier ones, virtually all of which seem certain to increase within the next year or two.

Louisiana Purchase Exposition glass paperweight with scene of Festival Hall $7.00

Louisiana Purchase Exposition metal drinking cups with etched scenes, pair $21.00

Louisiana Purchase Exposition official book of views, wrappers $5.00

Louisiana Purchase Exposition bronze medal $10.00

Louisiana Purchase Exposition dedication printed invitation $6.00

Louisiana Purchase Exposition silver-plated souvenir spoon $6.00

Louisiana Purchase Exposition silk badge with lithographed clasp $13.50

Pan-American Exposition souvenir booklet $10.00

Pan-American Exposition "Buffalo Dollar" $15.00

Pan-American Exposition encased 1901 Indian head cent $7.50

Pan-American Exposition glass paperweight $13.00

Pan-American Exposition playing cards $10.00

Panama-Pacific International Exposition napkin ring $5.00

Panama-Pacific International Exposition silver-plated spoon with bear on globe $6.00 to 8.50

Panama-Pacific International Exposition lead tray, 9×3½ inches $3.50

Panama-Pacific International Exposition Official Souvenir View Book $5.50

Panama-Pacific International Exposition watch fob $12.50

Philadelphia Centennial Exposition portfolio of views with fifty full-page lithographs $28.50

Philadelphia Centennial Exposition cast-iron Liberty Bell replica, 1 inch diameter $13.50

Philadelphia Centennial Exposition goblet with emblem $22.50

Philadelphia Centennial Exposition glass "Signers' Platter" $75.00

Philadelphia Centennial Exposition opaque glass Lincoln statuette $250.00

Philadelphia Centennial Exposition frosted lion paperweight $90.00

Philadelphia Centennial Exposition ironstone bread tray with transfer print of Horticultural Hall $90.00

Philadelphia Centennial Exposition "Centennalia" card game $8.50

Philadelphia Centennial Exposition medal, white metal $30.00

World's Columbian Exposition official medal, brass $5.00

World's Columbian Exposition bandanna, 22×24½ inches, pictorial designs and figures $25.00

World's Columbian Exposition egg-shaped salt shaker by Mt. Washington Glass Company $35.00

World's Columbian Exposition glass George Washington hatchet by Libby Glass Company $35.00 to 65.00

World's Columbian Exposition booklet, *Gems of the World's Fair* $7.50

World's Columbian Exposition ruby-flashed glass toothpick holder $18.00

World's Columbian Exposition *Official Directory* $6.50

World's Columbian Exposition commemorative half dollar $3.25

World's Columbian Exposition frosted-glass cat paperweight $85.00

World's Columbian Exposition "The World's Fair Game in Water Colors," with thirteen color prints by C. Graham $15.00

World's Columbian Exposition pilsner glass $25.00

World's Columbian Exposition silver witch plate by Daniel Low Company $60.00

SELECTED BIBLIOGRAPHY

THE BOOKS LISTED HERE deal primarily with the newer collectible objects. Many are still in print, and others will be found in the metropolitan public libraries. This bibliography is not intended to be exhaustive but to present a good cross-section of available books relating to many of the objects discussed in the preceding pages.

Andere, Mary. *Old Needlework Boxes and Their Tools: Their Story and How to Collect Them.* Drake Publishers, Ltd., New York.

Austen, Ferol. *The Poor Man's Guide to Bottle Collecting.* Doubleday & Company, Inc., Garden City, New York.

Battersby, Martin. *The Decorative Twenties.* Walker & Company, New York.

Bliven, Floyd E. *The Daguerreotype Story.* Vantage Press, New York

Bradford, Ernle. *English Victorian Jewellery.* Springs Books, Middlesex, England.

Bull, Peter, *Teddy Bear Book.* Random House, Inc., New York.

Burness, Tad. *Cars of the Early Twenties.* Chilton Book Company, Philadelphia.

Cleveland, Hugh. *Hugh Cleveland's Bottle Pricing Guide.* Cleveland Supply Company, San Angelo, Texas.

Cohen, Hal L. *Official Guide to Paper Americana,* H. C. Publishers, Inc., New York.

Colcleaser, Donald E. *Bottles: Yesterday's Trash, Today's Treasure.* Privately printed, Vallejo, California.

Cole, Ann Kilborn. *How to Collect the 'New Antiques.'* David McKay Company, Inc., New York.

Cope, Jim. *Soda Water Advertising.* Privately printed, Orange, Texas.

Daguerre, L. J. M. *An Historical and Descriptive Account of the Various Processes of the Daguerreotype and the Diorama by Daguerre* (facsimile reprint) Winter House, Ltd., New York.

Davis, Derek C., and Middlemas, Keith. *Colored Glass*. Clarkson N. Potter, Inc., New York.

Day, John. *Trains*. Grosset & Dunlap, New York.

DeVincenzo, Ralph (ed.). *Curios and Collectibles*. Dafran House Publishers, New York.

————. *Flea Market Shopper*. Dafran House Publishers, New York.

Flower, Margaret. *Victorian Jewellery*. A. S. Barnes & Company, Inc., South Brunswick, New Jersey.

Freeman, Larry. *Victorian Posters*. American Life Foundation, Watkins Glen, New York.

Georgana, G. N. (ed.) *Encyclopedia of American Automobiles* E. P. Dutton & Company, New York.

Gersheim, Helmut and Addison. *L. J. M. Daguerre*. World Publishing Company, Cleveland.

Goldstein, Shelly and Helen. *Coca-Cola Collectibles*. Privately published, Woodland Hills, California.

Gores, Stan. *1876 Centennial Collectibles and Price Guide*. Privately published, Fond du Lac, Wisconsin.

Hanson, Gary C. *The Handbook of American Bottles*. Privately published, Atlanta.

Hertz, Louis H. *Collecting Model Trains*. Mark Haber & Company, Wethersfield, Connecticut.

Hechtlinger, Adelaide. *The Great Patent Medicine Era, or Without Benefit of Doctor*. Grosset & Dunlap, New York.

Jenkins, Dorothy. *A Fortune in the Junk Pile*. Crown Publishers, Inc., New York.

Kendrick, Grace. *The Antique Bottle Collector*, 1971. Pyramid Publications, New York.

————. *The Mouth-Blown Bottle*. Privately printed, Fallon, Nevada.

Klamkin, Marian. *The Collector's Book of Bottles*. Dodd, Mead & Company, New York.

Klug, Ray. *Antique Advertising*. L. W. Promotions, Gas City, Indiana.

Kovel, Ralph and Terry. *The Complete Antiques Price List*. Crown Publishers, Inc., New York.

————. *Know Your Antiques*. Crown Publishers, Inc., New York.

————. *The Official Bottle Price List*. Crown Publishers, Inc., New York.

Lantz, Louise K. *Old American Kitchenware, 1725–1925*. Thomas Nelson, Inc., Camden, New Jersey, and Everybodys Press, Hanover, Pennsylvania.

McClinton, Katharine Morrison. *Antiques of American Childhood*. Clarkson N. Potter, Inc., New York.

————. *The Complete Book of Small Antiques Collecting*. Coward-McCann, Inc., New York.

Mebane, John. *Collecting Nostalgia*. Arlington House, New Rochelle, New York.

————. *The Coming Collecting Boom*. A. S. Barnes & Company, Inc., South Brunswick, New Jersey.

————. *New Horizons in Collecting: Cinderella Antiques*. A. S. Barnes & Company, Inc., South Brunswick, New Jersey.

————. *The Poor Man's Guide to Antique Collecting*. Doubleday & Company, Inc., Garden City, New York.

————. *Treasure at Home*. A. S. Barnes & Company, Inc., South Brunswick, New Jersey.

————. *What's New That's Old*. A. S. Barnes & Company, Inc., South Brunswick, New Jersey.

———— and Murphy, Catherine. *The Antique Trader Price Guide to Antiques and Collectors' Items*. Babka Publishing Company, Dubuque, Iowa.

Mosoriak, Roy. *The Curious History of Music Boxes*. Lightner Publishing Corporation, Chicago.

Munsey, Cecil. *The Illustrated Guide to Collecting Bottles*. Hawthorne Books, Inc., New York.

Newhall, Beaumont. *The Daguerreotype in America*. Duell, Sloan & Pearce, New York.

Orde-Hume, W. J. G. *Collecting Musical Boxes and How to Repair Them*. Crown Publishers, Inc., New York.

Rinhart, Floyd and Marion. *American Daguerrian Art*. Clarkson N. Potter, Inc., New York.

————. *American Miniature Case Art*. Clarkson N. Potter, Inc., New York.

Ruggles, Rowena Godding. *The One Rose, Mother of the Immortal Kewpies*. Privately printed, Oakland, California.

Schmeiser, Alan. *Have Bottles . . . Will Pop*. Michelan Press, Dixon, California.

Schroeder, Joseph J., Jr. (ed.). *The Wonderful World of Automobiles, 1895–1930*. Follett Publishing Company, Chicago.

Shull, Thelma. *Victorian Antiques*. Charles E. Tuttle Company, Rutland, Vermont.

Springer, L. Elsinore. *The Collector's Book of Bells*. Crown Publishers, Inc., New York.

Theofiles, George. *American Posters of World War I*. Dafran House, New York.

Tibbitts, John C. *John Doe, Bottle Collector*. The Little Glass Shack, Sacramento, California.

————. *1200 Bottles Priced*. The Little Glass Shack, Sacramento, California.

Tiffany Studios. *Ecclesiastical Department Brochure of Tiffany Studios*. Tiffany Studios, New York.

Toulouse, Julian Harrison. *Bottle Makers and Their Marks*. Thomas Nelson, Inc., Camden, New Jersey.

Towne, Morgan. *Treasures in Truck and Trash*. Doubleday & Company, Inc., Garden City, New York.

Turner, Noel D. *American Silver Flatware, 1837–1910*. A. S. Barnes & Company, South Brunswick, New Jersey.

Warman, Edwin D. *Twelfth Antiques and Their Current Prices*. E. G. Warman Publishing Company, Uniontown, Pennsylvania.

Watson, Richard. *Bitters Bottles*. Thomas Nelson, Inc., Camden, New Jersey.

Wilson, Bill and Betty. *19th Century Medicine in Glass*. 19th Century Hobby & Publishing Company, Amador City, California.

————. *Spirits Bottles of the Old West*. B & B Enterprises, Santa Rosa, California.

Wise, David Burgess. *Vintage Motorcars*. Grosset & Dunlap, New York.

Ziel, Ron. *The Twilight of the Steam Locomotives*. Grosset & Dunlap, New York.

INDEX